ACCEPTED

ACCEPTED

*How the First Gay Superstar
Changed WWE*

Pat Patterson

with Bertrand Hébert

Published by ECW Press
665 Gerrard Street East, Toronto, ON M4M 1Y2
416-694-3348 / info@ecwpress.com

"Goodbye My Friend" written by Karla Bonoff, courtesy of Seagrape Music.

"My Way"
English Words by Paul Anka
Original French Words by Gilles Thibault
Music by Jacques Revaux and Claude Francois
Copyright © 1967 Societe Des Nouvelles and Editions Eddie Barclay
Copyright © 1969 Chrysalis Standards, Inc., Songs Music Publishing, LLC and iWay Holdings SAS
Copyright Renewed
All Rights for Chrysalis Standards, Inc. Administered by BMG Rights Management (US) LLC
All Rights for iWay Holdings SAS Administered by Songs Music Publishing, LLC
All Rights Reserved Used by Permission
Reprinted by Permission of Hal Leonard Corporation

To the best of his abilities, the author has related experiences, places, people, and organizations from his memories of them. In order to protect the privacy of others, he has, in some instances, changed the names of certain people and details of events and places.

The statements and opinions expressed in this work are solely those of the author and do not reflect the views of WWE. WWE hereby disclaims any responsibility for such statements and opinions, and they should not be construed as representing WWE's position on any subject.

WWE would like to thank GLAAD for its support and valued feedback in the development of *Accepted*.

Library and Archives Canada Cataloguing in Publication

Patterson, Pat, 1941–, author
Accepted : how the first gay superstar changed WWE / Pat Patterson with Bertrand Hébert ; foreword by Vincent K. McMahon.

Issued in print and electronic formats.
ISBN 978-1-77041-293-4 (hardback); ISBN 978-1-77090-863-5 (PDF); ISBN 978-1-77090-864-2 (ePub)
ISBN 978-1-77041-377-1 (signed edition)

1. Patterson, Pat, 1941–. 2. Wrestlers—Canada—Biography. 3. Gay athletes—Canada—Biography. 4. Wrestling—United States. 5. World Wrestling Entertainment, Inc. I. Hébert, Bertrand, 1971–, author II. Title.

GV1196.P38A3 2016   796.812092   C2016-902329-X
C2016-902330-3

Editor for the press: Michael Holmes
Cover image: Bob Cartago
Interior images: Unless otherwise stated, photos are from the author's personal collection or WWE's archives.

Printed and bound at Friesens
in Canada   5   4   3   2   1

MIX
Paper from
responsible sources
FSC
www.fsc.org   FSC® C016245

This book is dedicated to the memory of Louie Dondero.
You made me the man I was, and you gave me the opportunity to be the man
I am. Thanks for being there. I will always love you, my friend.

FOREWORD

I've had the privilege to have Pat Patterson as my best friend for over forty years, so I am truly honored to have been a part of his remarkable life and to write this foreword.

Pat's passion to perform began very early in life. The fourth of nine children, Pat grew up in the poorest neighborhood in Montreal. It was a difficult childhood, but Pat never stopped dreaming of the big time. In 1960, at the age of nineteen, Pat borrowed money from his sister for a bus ticket to Boston. With just twenty dollars in his pocket and speaking no English at all, Pat finagled his way into joining a local wrestling organization, and the rest is history. Pat went on to become one of the greatest superstars of all time, selling out Madison Square Garden and arenas all over the world.

Pat Patterson's path to stardom had obstacles most of us could not even imagine today. Despite his extraordinary work ethic, his passion, his loyalty, and his integrity, Pat Patterson was different in an era when "different" was not something to be celebrated. While some people persecuted and humiliated him for his sexual orientation, Pat persevered and eventually earned the respect of everyone he ever met and worked with, including his life partner of forty years Louis Dondero, as well as Bret Hart, Shawn Michaels, André the Giant, and the great French Canadian Maurice Vachon. Notably, Pat would come to mentor a young man who would later become known as "The Rock."

Pat's stellar in-ring career came to an end in 1984 — but an equally impressive career began when he joined WWE as an executive. If not for the magnificent creative mind of Pat Patterson, I can honestly say WWE would not be anywhere near where it is today. Pat Patterson will always have my undying respect and admiration. I hope you enjoy his life story as much as I have enjoyed being a part of his life.

— Vincent Kennedy McMahon
February 2016

ACCEPTED

INTRODUCTION

Even after all these years, and all my travels, I never thought I would find myself writing a book. It's my life — and it felt pretty normal to me. People who know me, however, have always said, "Pat, you ought to write a goddamn book. The life that you have had is amazing."

As time went on, they got me seriously thinking about this project. And you know what? When I look back at my life, it *is* amazing that I'm still here doing what I love. After all, my friend Louie and I were almost killed in a car wreck before the whole thing even got rolling.

Still, I didn't want to write a book to "put myself over," to tell you how many championships I've won, or how great my wrestling matches were. I know some fans like that stuff, not that there is anything wrong with that, but most of it can be found with the simple click of a button. Why write a book about that? Most fans I meet today know more about my career than I do. Yet Vince McMahon himself kept telling me I should do it. "It's a great story, Patrick," he said.

Though wrestling will always be a part of my life, I always felt that my life was a lot more than just that. In fact, it was something entirely different from my career. Wrestling has never been the be-all and end-all of my life, even when I was headlining Madison Square Garden four times in a row against Bob Backlund for the WWE Championship. But people ask me, "How did you get here?" and when I seriously thought about my life and what I have accomplished, I realized that there might just be a story worth telling. I've laughed, loved, experienced sadness, and lived incredible adventures with wonderful people along the way.

How *did* I get here? How did a poor French Canadian kid, who didn't speak English (some people say I still don't, by the way) become what I've become? I didn't have a master plan when I left home to wrestle in Boston; I didn't know then that I was an artist trying to find a way to express himself. My life has been a never-ending story — I understand that now — and I love telling stories. But where to start, when there have been enough shenanigans for two lifetimes?

I even stopped being a wrestler at Vince McMahon's request and became a senior vice president who worked in an *office* — and I had quit school so I would never have to work in an office. Funny, how life throws you curve balls. I still have no idea what a senior vice president does, but I know wrestling. That's still what I do today.

Here I am again, talking about wrestling, no closer to figuring out how to start my book . . .

But if you're still with me after all this rambling, then I think you and I will have some fun. I, for one, cannot wait to go on this trip down memory lane, as I try to figure out how I went from sharing a bed with my brother to staying in the fanciest hotel suites in the world while working for WWE.

Wait a minute, that's it. I know where I need to go to tell my story.

It all started in Montréal, more than fifty-eight years ago . . .

MONTRÉAL

"For what is a man, what has he got?
If not himself, then he has naught"

I was born on January 19, 1941, in Montréal, in a tiny apartment
near the corner of Frontenac on Rouen Street, in the Ville-Marie
borough. Back then, it was known as the *Faubourg à m'lasse*, the sub-
urb of molasses. That is to say, the people were poor and ate a lot of
molasses. I don't really remember it that way, but that's where I grew
up — and we sure did eat a lot of molasses.

My father's name was Gérard Clermont, and he was a good
provider, though I was never particularly close to him. My mother,
Simone Lupien, was the most wonderful mom anyone could have
had. I was very close to her; she was the only member of my family
who understood me from the start and always accepted me as I am.

My mom took care of our family of eleven, while my dad worked
as a milkman. He would walk to work at 3 a.m. and pick up his horse
and carriage at the stable to start his deliveries. People would leave
two empty bottles on the front porch and Dad would leave them
two full. He did that 365 days a year, no matter the weather — even

through Montréal's frigid and snowy winters. He did the same thing every day to provide for us. Later he worked in the shop at Canadair, building plane parts, and it was a good, secure job. That's not to say being a milkman wasn't a good job back then, it just didn't pay as well. All his life, my dad sacrificed a lot for us.

I had four brothers and four sisters. The first born was André. My mother lost a second child, though we only learned about that fairly recently. My father then proceeded to make sure my mother was pregnant on a regular basis: Claudette, Suzanne, Pierre, Normand, Lise, Annette, Michel, and finally Richard.

If you are wondering, I'm the Pierre on that list, Pierre Clermont. God, I hated that name. It was so common. Everyone around me was a Clermont. I wanted to be different and unique. Later, I changed it to Pat Patterson — but we'll get to that, don't worry.

Let me be blunt: my childhood was awful. I feel worse about it today than I did back then when I didn't know any better. We had a two-bedroom apartment; one was for my parents, and the other had six of us sleeping in it — one bed with two children and one bunk bed with two more on each level. Six people sharing a tiny room barely bigger than the bathroom in most hotel rooms I stay in today.

Me? I wasn't lucky enough to have my sleeping quarters in a bedroom.

There was a little hallway when you came into the apartment, and at the end of this hallway was a small closet. Inside we had a folding bed; you had to fold and hide it every morning and take it out of there before going to bed at night. I slept in that bed right in the hallway with my brother Normand. You can imagine how much fun that was. When someone wanted something from the closet, they had to take the whole bed out. Richard, the youngest, slept in the kitchen on another folding bed. He was always the last one to go to sleep, even if he was tired the earliest, as he had to wait for everyone else to go to bed.

(From left to right) Normand, Claudette, André, Suzanne, and me. Annette, Mom, Dad, and Lise. Finally, Richard and Michel.

Can you imagine that? I lived it and I almost can't believe it was real. As a small child, I was already living in the closet. There was never any room anywhere in that place and never any privacy. It was crazy. There was no way to be alone with yourself, if you know what I mean.

Still, we were lucky we lived on the third floor of a building owned by my grandmother on my father's side. There were two apartments beside each other on each floor. My uncle and my aunt were our downstairs neighbors, and on the first floor was my grandmother. Beside us was a couple with one child in the same amount of space that we had for eleven; we thought they were living the life of the rich and famous. When that family finally moved out, a year or two before I left the house, we removed our restroom, broke through the wall, and created one big apartment for us.

There was no bath, no shower, and no hot water. Any time we needed hot water, we had to boil it, even to wash our hands. You could only get so clean like that, as you couldn't be naked in the middle of the kitchen in front of everyone. Imagine it: eleven people washing up one after the other. "Who's next?"

In Montréal, we had public baths since most apartments didn't have hot water. The baths were where real personal hygiene took place. Ours was called Bain Quintal. All that's left of those establishments today are a few public swimming pools. Twice a week, my mom would give us a little piece of soap and we would go there by foot, at least a thirty-minute walk. Few people had cars back then, and certainly not my family. At Bain Quintal, there was a guard posted at the entrance who would yell, "*As-tu du savon?*" *Do you have soap?*

(Pardon my French, but it is my first language and I still use it today. It feels more authentic to keep some of it in my story. Don't worry, I will use my best English to translate.)

"*Oui!*" we would answer in unison.

"*Vas-te laver,*" he would shout back. *Go wash yourself.*

We were always dirty. Going to the public baths twice a week was not enough. As alien as the concept of public baths might seem today, it was fun for us because after we bathed, we went in the pool to swim. The guard would make sure we had cleaned ourselves properly in the shower before being allowed to use the pool. My mother

My loving mother, Simone, and my dad, Gérard.

would give us a towel with that little piece of soap. And she would remind us all the time, *"Rapporte le savon." Bring back the soap.*

Ain't that something? That's how poor we were: not even a whole bar of soap and we had to bring it back home with us.

My mother made sure nothing was ever wasted. If she cooked ground beef, do you think she would throw away the leftover grease? Oh no, she would use it to cook something else. We were poor, but we never missed anything truly necessary, and there was always something to eat. There was only one mealtime, however, and if you missed it, you wouldn't get anything else. Dessert every weeknight was molasses, and on weekends, we would be treated with two cookies each. Sometimes, at Christmas, my mother would buy a cake or make one. It was the best — a real treat. With eleven of us, it never lasted long; once we each got a piece, there was rarely anything left.

When we were all going to school, my mom could not keep up with the chores. We had a small place but my mom needed help. My parents took my oldest sister, Claudette, out of school when she was sixteen, so she could help at home. Even today I need to remind her that she's not my mother. Don't get me wrong, I love her dearly, but she was quite young to be given so much responsibility. It still affects her. She helped our mother with washing our clothes, cooking meals, and cleaning. She spent four or five years helping my mom like that. Then she got a boyfriend and a job, and the next sister in line took her place. They learned everything from my mom, so when they decided to get married, they knew how to take care of their home. Things were like that back then.

I was never really close to anyone in my family except for my mother. Looking back, it seems like I was never living in the same world as everyone else. I think my reality was always different.

I never had the chance to know my paternal grandfather — he passed away when I was very young — but, by all accounts, he was the person most like me in my family. He was a creator, kind of like me in a sense. Our apartment building was right beside the school and the church, and a lot of people passed by every day bustling from one place to the next. My grandfather made something that made people stop, that they just could not believe: a giant spinning Christmas tree with blinking lights. It was unheard of in the early forties, and people would stand in front of our house admiring the tree in the window for ages. My grandmother had her hands full with the youngest of her own children, so I barely had time to get know her but the stories she told me about my grandfather still fascinate me. The man built a pool table by himself from scratch. He even handcrafted the balls from wood. He must have been an amazing, creative soul. People were very ingenious back then, but it was more than that with him. My grandfather would invent things. Everyone who knew him told me he was a genius. I wish I could have known him; I feel we would have a lot to talk about.

The one luxury we had was a radio set, and it was very important to the whole family, and me especially. Listening to music on the radio, I could escape reality. I would listen to *Les découvertes de Billy Munro* (my best translation would be *Billy Munro's Discoveries*). I liked that show a lot. Today, one of my favorite television shows is *America's Got Talent* — a very similar concept. My dad later bought a mechanical piano, which played music by itself. I could have listened to it forever.

When I was young, all my friends played hockey. But not me. I practiced figure skating. During the winter, there was an ice rink in almost every park in the city. I had girls' skates, bought at the Salvation Army, which I painted black. I was doing all the fancy stuff you could imagine and even performed duet routines with girls. I wanted everyone to watch me. This is probably the first time some- one called me a "faggot." In French, the word is *tapette*. I didn't let it

Christmas memories with my family are not all great.

bother me: I really didn't know what it meant, or even who I was yet. In those days, that kind of thing happened and there wasn't much we could do about being called names. Today someone like me could end up going to the Olympics, but back then I was everyone's laughingstock. Still, I had a crowd in front of me, so I was in heaven. I loved it enough that I went to see the Ice Capades or the Ice Follies (I'm not sure which) in the hopes of auditioning with the troupe. They told me I was too young. I must have been thirteen or fourteen.

In my family, as for a lot of French Canadian Catholic families, Christmas was only for Mass and the baby Jesus; gifts were exchanged on New Year's. We went to Mass again on December 31, but when we got back, gifts were waiting for us on the kitchen table. It wasn't ever much, and many years we got a few pairs of new socks and things like that.

I remember one year I had seen what they called *la machine à vue* in a store — a projector that would let us watch a film on the wall or on a white sheet. You could even rent 8mm movies to create your own little cinema at home. I really wanted one, but my dad made it clear we didn't need it. My father didn't change his mind easily, so I gave up and forgot about it. Well, guess what was on the table with all the gifts when we returned home from church? *La machine à vue!* I jumped on it and told my dad thank you. I was overjoyed! But then came the crushing words: "It's not for you."

I was devastated. It was for my brother Normand. I got a toboggan that year. What was I going to do with that? I didn't like sports, except for skating. I was so disappointed. My brother couldn't care less about *la machine à vue,* but Normand would rarely let me play with it because it was his gift. My dad explained to me that my brother had better results in school than I did and that's why he was rewarded with the movie machine. It was the only time I wished I'd had good grades. Since I hated school, I was neither good nor bad at it, I just didn't try.

I ended up using the machine just a handful of times; most of the time it was my dad who used it, not Normand. Dad would invite everyone to my grandmother's and he would rent Laurel and Hardy or Abbott and Costello movies — all physical humor since the machine didn't have sound. Me, I would put on a big show for my friends, setting up a sheet in the back alley, and by the time it was dark, I had drawn a full house. If that thing had been mine, I could have built an empire. My brother recently told me he doesn't know why Dad ever gave him *la machine à vue* — he never wanted it.

My brother and I can laugh about it now, even though that was not the only time I felt left out. My dad would never give me any money, while Normand could get almost anything he wanted. They related to each other through sports. He would get a dollar for each time he scored a goal, a fortune back in those days. What you have to understand, and what I've only just recently realized, is that my brother had been sick as a kid and one of his legs was paralyzed for a while. My dad went to church every night to pray for him. And not just to our regular church, but to Saint Joseph's Oratory of Mount Royal, the most famous shrine in Montréal, known for its miracles. My dad would climb all the stairs of this place on his knees in the hope that my brother would walk normally once again. The leg did heal up and Normand became an athlete. It really was a kind of miracle. Dad was so happy about it and so proud of my brother. I can only imagine the joy of a parent when one of their kids can overcome something like that. It just shows you how bad we were at communicating. I've come to realize that my dad loved me, but that he just couldn't find a way to connect with me. We were not on the same page, that's for sure. It took me thirty years to figure this out.

2

THE ROAR OF
THE PAINT AND THE
SMELL OF THE CROWD

"I planned each charted course, each careful step along the byway"

While my brother Normand was good at sports, I was a mess. I tried different things but never really found my way. Back in those days, there were traveling circuses, going from town to town, and when they were nearby, I spent all my free time there. I would hang around the acrobats even though I didn't speak one word of English. One time, one of the acrobats let me climb up a pole to the top, 100 feet above the ground. I did a few swings — and a few falls in the net. I was on cloud nine. The next day, I pointed out the pole to my dad; we could see it from our home. I said I was going to the top, because I wanted him to see me perform. My dad went berserk. He was beside himself, probably scared to death for me, and he proceeded to squash my circus aspirations right there. If I had had more guts in that moment, I would have left home to join the circus to become a clown or an acrobat. I would have done anything, even swept the floor, just to run away and find something that would make me happy.

Instead, I just kept on looking. There was an amateur singing contest held at bars called *Les découvertes de Jean Simon*. We didn't have reality television back then, but a lot of Montréal artists became stars at these places. I wanted to do it so badly, but Jean Simon told me that since I was my mid-teens, I was too young to sing in bars. I bugged him so much that he helped me get in through the back door to sing my song and leave right away, so no one would get in trouble. I don't know why, but every night he would let me sing my song. I was so happy. I had an audience and an orchestra, even if I was really not very good. I needed to feel the audience reacting to me. One day, I told my dad about the singing contest. Once again, he squashed my dreams and my aspirations by forbidding me to do it ever again. I had been hoping he would bring everyone to hear me sing. But he was clueless; he never got me.

After that, I did it behind his back. I even tried out for my favorite show *Les découvertes de Billy Munro*, which aired on the radio every Sunday morning. I basically just impersonated a famous local singer called Jen Roger. He was my hero; nobody remembers him today, but back then in my eyes he was the biggest star. When they heard me audition, they threw me out: I was just an imitator. I didn't let that stop me. He was my hero and a major celebrity, and I found out where Jen Roger would eat on Sainte Catherine Street. Back then, most restaurants had shows while you ate. I asked the stage manager if I could sing my song. I actually got an ovation and even Jen Roger applauded me. In 2012, some fifty years later, they had a big birthday celebration for Jen Roger in a theater. I was invited to sing. There were dozens of singers from the province of Québec all singing their best stuff for him. They all went before me, so I was torturing myself to find a way to top them.

I was putting more pressure on myself than if I was having a WWE Championship match with Bob Backlund at Madison Square Garden.

Jen Roger was sitting there, in a wheelchair, with all of his friends facing the stage. So I started by saying, "I've always loved Jen Roger and when I was young, you were my hero. I loved you so much and I am going to tell you a story." I reminded him about singing his song so many years earlier, but I added that he actually went to the bathroom when I started. As expected, everyone started laughing and I got the reaction I was looking for — a pop, as we refer to it in the ring. I then looked straight at him and said, "You better not stand up and go to the bathroom this time."

Now everyone was laughing so hard they could hardly breathe. I sang the Elvis song "The Wonder of You." It went very well. It felt so good doing that, because he'd been such an inspiration.

Today, it's clear to me that when I was a kid I was always looking for an audience. There was a church where they did a passion play every year during Easter. In the part after Jesus died, where everyone on stage was praying, there was always a big rock in the middle of the stage. Behind it, the curtain was slightly open. Then Jesus would suddenly appear from behind the rock and begin to levitate. It wasn't very high, but it really intrigued me. I wanted to know how they did it. I *needed* to know. But I wasn't allowed to go backstage. I still found a way, thinking, *The hell with what I can or can't do.* Do you know what it was? It was a simple seesaw that you can find in almost any park today — a child's toy. Jesus was standing on one end and someone pushed him up. The rock made the illusion come to life for the audience. It was amazing. I wanted to amaze people like that. And in a sense, that's what I did in my wrestling career.

After that I built my own stage with some friends and we played the Passion of Christ. I played Jesus. Backstage one day, the girl who

An altar boy at church; I loved playing priest at home.

14

played Mary and I became curious about the differences in our anatomy . . . But that's another story — and it went nowhere, as you could probably guess.

The only constant in my childhood was that I was always trying to create a show and get a crowd to come out and watch. No matter what kind of a performer you are, what drives you is not the promise of a big audience, but *any* audience — no matter the size. I could sing in my house all day long, it would feel good. But it would be nicer to have someone listening to me.

My father was very religious, as I've said. Every Sunday, we *had* to go to church. Not that we were the only ones: every Sunday, everybody in the province of Québec *had* to go to church. So, I went to Mass often and, strangely, I used to love it. I loved to watch the priest preaching and to look at the people listening to him, all dressed up, as he made them stand or kneel almost at will. The priest was a star. Mass was the first show I ever saw. I loved it so much that I became an altar boy; I wanted to be a part of the ceremony. For a while, I went to Mass every morning before school and was paid five cents for each Mass. Don't laugh, five cents went a long way back then. I could get two hot dogs for that.

Eventually I was on duty for all the funerals and all the weddings. I loved it like crazy — I was on stage in front of people every day. In fact, I loved it so much that I built an altar in my grandmother's yard and started playing priest. I even had a real costume given to me by an old priest. They used to say that May was the month of Mary (it still is, but they just don't say it as much anymore) and at 7 p.m. every night in May we had to get on our knees either at church or at home and say the rosary. In my house, my father insisted that everyone had to be there when we did this. Each evening, one of us led the family in the prayer. Sometimes we would go outside to my altar to say the rosary and some neighbors would join us. I invited our priest to come and see my altar, and the day he said he was coming, I told everyone that the priest would be there to say the rosary with me. When he showed up, there must have been 200 people in our yard. Afterward, I was basking in my new fame. Everyone was talking about it. They were all there to see me perform. I had found what I was looking for without even realizing it.

We also had to go to confession in those days. There was no joking around and I hated that part. The first time I went, I told the priest I had masturbated.

"Please don't do that, my son; it's a sin. As a penance, I want you to wash your hands with holy water," he told me.

The second time I went to confession, I told my sin to the priest. He said, "As a penance, I want you to drink holy water."

I'm just kidding. Lighten up, will you? Laugh a little.

I will get to that soon enough.

Though the priesthood wasn't my true calling, for a brief moment, I thought I might just become a priest. After I found out that would require going to school for a long time, any aspiration I had to consecrate my life to the church ended. On top of the fact that I hated school, the cost of tuition made it impossible to seriously consider.

At that time in Québec, the Catholic Church was almost more powerful than our elected officials. We could not eat meat on Fridays, and I didn't like fish or eggs. Most of us poor people ate *galette de sarrasin*, a buckwheat pancake, or hot dog buns (without sausages). I remember that the restriction made my mother's life even more difficult as she had to figure out how to feed us without meat.

For one of those Fridays without meat, my mom bought a loaf of bread and inside the bag was a ticket to see a wrestling show on a Saturday afternoon. I wasn't sure what the show was — we didn't have a television set at the time — but it was free, so I was going no matter what. We could not afford to see any shows then. I went crazy after seeing my first match, and I have yet to fully recover.

I remember watching Buddy Rogers enter the ring. It was like God was walking down the aisle. He had a presence about him; I didn't know what he was made of. It was incredible, and I've never seen anything like it since — this slow, easy wrestling with Édouard Carpentier. My God, it was so beautiful. Years later, I wrestled with both of them and became friends with Rogers.

I knew after that first wrestling match that I had found my calling, but I needed money to attend the big shows on Saturday nights or the even bigger show at the Montréal Forum on Wednesday evenings. One of my friends had a delivery job for a little restaurant and I helped him and he paid me for my work. He also delivered newspapers, and I helped with that too and earned some more money there as well. It wasn't much, but it was enough to see the wrestling show.

When I watched the Dufresne Brothers wrestle, I hated their guts. The bad guys, they were so mean and dirty. I cheered for the heroes such as Sam Chuck and Joe White. Good guys versus bad guys: I was hooked. And fans got mad for real as they screamed, "Goddamn ref, he just pulled his hair, you dumb bastard!" One day I saw the real stars: Killer Kowalski and Yvon Robert at the Forum. Yvon Robert was so much more than a wrestler to French Canadians in those days. He was a true role model, proof we could succeed even if we only spoke French.

Since I didn't have enough money to go as often as I'd like, I also got creative. If people left the show at intermission, I would ask for their ticket stub and watch the second half of the show for free. Sometimes, someone would let me in to the famed Forum; other times, the ushers would check out the action and I would jump the pay-gate while they were distracted.

I think the first job I ever did in the wrestling business was sell hot dogs. I was not good at that at all, since all I wanted to do was to watch the matches. Once, one of the wrestlers asked me to get near the barricades for his match so he could turn the hot dog tray over my head. I was happy to comply, because it meant I wouldn't have any more hot dogs to sell and I could watch the rest of the matches without working. My boss didn't see it that way. He fired me. It didn't matter to me: I wanted more of the kind of crowd reaction I experienced when I was showered with hot dogs, mustard, and ketchup.

I was crazy for wrestling. It took over an hour to walk to the Forum, and it was the same to get back after the show. I even went in the winter. During a snowstorm, I would stop on Saint Laurent Street on my way home, *la main* as we called it, where everything was happening back in those days. There was this newspaper stand on Saint Laurent and when it was cold like that, the man stayed inside the stand and left an old cigar box outside for people to drop their five cents in for a paper. I would fake putting some money in and take out twenty-five cents "in change." Then I used that quarter to buy two hot dogs, French fries, and a Coke and warm myself in the restaurant, so I could get home without losing a significant part of my anatomy to frostbite. That happened quite often, and I would like to thank that man for keeping me strong and warm by allowing me, without his knowledge, to eat before finishing my long walk home in the snow.

If I could get to a show early, I would wait where stars like Yvon Robert and Buddy Rogers parked their cars and offer to help bring their stuff inside — in an attempt to get in to the Forum for free.

"Can I carry suitcase?" I would ask in my limited English.

Killer Kowalski gave me his bag once, and I got in with him. That didn't happen too often, mind you, but I felt like I was on top of the world that night.

When I started to wrestle, I patterned my whole look after him — with my purple trunks and boots. I wanted a picture of me coming off the top rope with the big knee just like Kowalski, the move with which, in 1956 at the Forum, he tore off Yukon Eric's ear. When I finally got that picture, all I wanted was to show it to Kowalski and have him sign it. Many times, I tried to get close to him and get it autographed without success. I was always sniffing around trying to get as close as possible to the dressing room, so I could show him my precious picture. Finally one day, I had my chance. I was about to get kicked out of the dressing room when Kowalski showed up at the door.

"What do you want, kid?"

I held up the picture and was so proud to ask him in my best English ever, "You autograph, please?"

If he had handed me back a gold bar, I would not have been happier. I still have the autographed photo today, and it's one of the few pieces of wrestling memorabilia that has value to me. I get emotional thinking about it. Later on, I became good friends with Kowalski, working together in Australia and Japan. I'm proud of that and still find it amazing that I went from a wannabe wrestler to wrestling with one of my idols.

Anyway, at that time I was still in school but, as I explained, I never found anything for me there — there was no drama class or anything like that for me. I got a diploma after seven years of grade school and that was it. I was already dreaming about wrestling. I had already started to train around age fourteen at Les Loisirs Saint Jean Baptiste, going there once or twice a week. I don't remember who trained me, some old-timer who taught me the basics, but I remember loving it right away. Everything came easily to me. The guy showed me something and I could do it almost right away. Another sign that I had found my calling.

I found out that one of my school classmates was the son of the wrestling promoter Sylvio Samson. He didn't have a television show, but he drew some nice crowds, especially during the summer. Let me tell you, it didn't take me long to become friends with his son. I started to also train with some old-timers at Le Palais des Sports where Samson held his matches. They stretched me more than they really taught me. They had me in pain all the time. I learned how to fall and how to run the ropes — they'd at least shown me that.

But over at Loisirs, I hooked up with three other trainees and we were good together. I had my first match in 1958. Then one night, I was wrestling with Fred Sauvé who was the biggest wrestler at Loisirs. Someone had left a Coke bottle ringside, so when I took a bump outside, on a whim I grabbed it and I broke it on the ring post. I proceeded to go back in the ring with the broken bottle. Everyone jumped on me including the priest, who was in charge of everything because Loisirs was part of his parish. I was so believable they were sure I was going to use it against my opponent. People who had paid twenty-five cents to see the show were getting a good one. I got kicked out of Les Loisirs for that move. Imagine: my career was nearly over before it even started.

Thank God I had secretly been training at Le Palais des Sports with Cyclone Samson, the promoter's son. He didn't want his dad to find out he was wrestling, because his dad didn't want him to enter the business. But I was meeting Sylvio Samson, a very stern and serious man, on a very regular basis. One day I finally decided to admit to him that we had been training.

"*What?* You're not going to drag my son into the wrestling business, you little bastard!"

And so I ended up back at the Loisirs. Pat Girard had begun working there shortly after I was kicked out, and he knew I could already wrestle. He was a big star in Europe — he even wrestled in

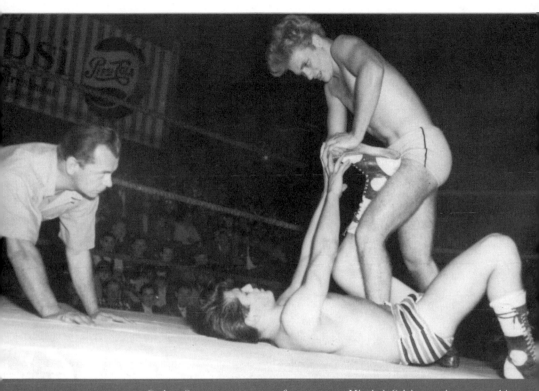

Cyclone Samson was my very first opponent. His dad, Sylvio, was instrumental in getting my career started. Photo courtesy of Sylvain Samson and family.

front of the Queen of England as Pat Curry — and became a well-known trainer for most of the wrestlers who came out of Montréal until the Loisirs shut down in 1990. It's a funny thing: people know I learned wrestling at the Loisirs, so everyone assumes Pat Girard trained me. But I started at Les Loisirs before Pat Girard started wrestling there. By the time I went back, I had already wrestled my first match, so I can't really call him my teacher, although I did wrestle at the Loisirs for him.

But, again, I didn't stay there long. I went back again to Sylvio Samson and pled the case that he should give his son and me a chance to work together on one of his shows. He finally relented and gave us the opener in Saint Jérôme, a town just outside Montréal. I gave everything I had to Cyclone that night as he was drop-kicking me to the moon. The old man went apeshit about how good we were. I made his son shine and look like the world champion. After that, Cyclone and I wrestled everywhere together. He was winning every night, but I couldn't care less. The older wrestlers saw what I was doing and they liked me right away. Bear in mind I was only seventeen. Then I started to get paired up with more experienced talent; they wanted to wrestle with me because of all those bumps I was taking.

When I started in the business, I was 190 pounds and around 5 foot 10. Let me tell you, I drank a lot protein shakes, trying to get bigger. (I was not a big fan of the gym.) I was ready to do anything I needed to in order to succeed in the business. Nothing would stop me.

While working for promoter Sylvio Samson, we went everywhere in the province of Québec. That's when Maurice "Mad Dog" Vachon first noticed me and started to take an interest.

"Toé, tu vas faire un bon lutteur!" You're going to be a good wrestler, he said to me one day. He wasn't telling everyone, but he kept encouraging me. And no matter what, he was still scaring the hell out of me. I saw him once in the dressing room with one of his friends, who was the shits as a wrestler, and the guy was driving Maurice crazy. He kept badgering Mad Dog about their plans for the night, and Maurice kept on asking to be left alone. Maurice got mad and just beat the crap out of him right there and then in the dressing room. I didn't want to be anywhere near Mad Dog Vachon — that's how scared I was.

I also worked for Claude Desharnais, who would promote towns for Sylvio that were farther away from Montréal. If the town was near the end of the known world, you could be sure Desharnais was promoting there. We were making five dollars a night at best. We had nothing left when we came back from those godforsaken trips. The expenses on the road ate away at any profit. One time, there were seven of us in a car — two in the front, three in the back, and two little people as well. At least I was learning how to wrestle and gaining valuable experience while having fun. I entertained myself on those long trips, since I was getting broke traveling. I loved playing ribs as far back as I can remember. In Montréal, we would light the dressing room's trashcan on fire during the main event and then leave. When my friends would come back after their match, there was so much smoke, they almost could not get in. We used to pull shit like that all the time. Today, in WWE, we can't do that as it stirs up way too much trouble way too quickly.

While I was working for Desharnais and Samson, and even for my first match in 1958 at the Loisirs, I was always billed under the name of Pat Patterson. Could you imagine me coming to the ring as "Pierre Clermont"? That just doesn't work. The Smith Brothers were a couple of guys who wrestled for Samson doing a lumberjack gimmick. One of them was Pat Smith. I liked that name Pat, but I just couldn't find the right name to go with it. So I looked at the back of a dictionary, the proper nouns section, closed my eyes, and opened it randomly. First thing I saw when I opened my eyes was Patterson. I never looked back, and no promoter ever tried to change my name.

I made my fame under that name and back then, nothing was difficult about using a different name. No one asked questions — not even getting a driver's license was a problem.

Around 2009, I finally got around to changing my name legally. Everyone always called me Pat Patterson; even my own family had made the switch. Thank God, because they used to call me *Pierrot*, little Pierre. Pierrot had been gone for so long, it was about time they stopped calling me that. Pierre Clermont never really existed. In a sense, I think I was always Pat Patterson, you know what I mean?

At any rate, I went to see a lawyer to become an American citizen. I already had a green card after years of working in the United States. But even though I had been living in the country for most of my life, and I was already paying my taxes to Uncle Sam, if anything happened, I could still be kicked out and then I would not be able to work for WWE anymore. I felt I needed to become a citizen. It all went very smoothly and I became a U.S. citizen. Now that that was done, I could legally change my name.

It was not quite like regular court. There were about ten or fifteen of us with our lawyers, waiting for our turn. The judge didn't take the proceedings lightly. If something was wrong with the paperwork, people were dismissed for the day. I was the last one for the day and I was a little scared when my turn came. I didn't want to have to start all over again and wait for another court appointment. I can still hear the judge asking me, "Why do you want to change your name? It's a nice name, Pierre Clermont."

I told him, "Well, it's not a great name for wrestling, Your Honor. I have been using Pat Patterson since I was a teenage kid."

"Did you ever wrestle Dick the Bruiser and Pat O'Connor?" he asked.

I said, "Yeah, I did."

"I used to love those guys."

So the judge, who had been scaring me all day, started to talk wrestling with me. It was unbelievable. At the end, he said, "No more Pierre Clermont."

He stamped everything and he sent me on my way to get all of my paperwork done in the building across the street. Fifteen minutes later, everything was done.

Pierre Clermont was gone for good.

3

STRAIGHT OUT OF MONTRÉAL

"My friend, I'll say it clear, I'll state my case, of which I'm certain"

When I first started to get paid for wrestling, promoters occasionally paid me by check. Because I was still very young and had no bank account, my dad cashed my checks for me. And, of course, those checks sometimes bounced. He would go crazy, telling me I should quit "that goddamn wrestling" and that people were taking advantage of me. He forced me to get a "real" job.

Well, I soon discovered I wasn't cut out for traditional employment.

My first job was at a shoe factory. I would pile up boxes of shoes in the warehouse. I stuck it out for six or seven months, before I got pissed at everyone and told them to go to hell.

My dad was mad. *"Tabarnak, tu peux pas garder une job."* Goddamn *it, you can't keep a job.* He berated me, and I had nothing to say in my defense. I just hated working there.

After that, I went to work in a cookie factory. I lasted a month this time. I needed freedom. My boss was a crazy woman and we had a terrible relationship from the get-go. Cookies weren't for me either.

I wanted to do what I wanted to do — I couldn't work in that type of environment where each minute is counted, where no one laughs, and where people blame you to save their own asses. If I hadn't found wrestling, I might have become a thief or something equally socially unacceptable, just so I could escape and have some fun.

Still, I was a good son and kept looking for the proverbial "real" job. I made at least twenty applications to a cigarette factory called Macdonald, which is still standing in Montréal today. If they hired you, it was for life, and you'd get a great retirement plan. We lived right next door. I went in almost every day to apply. The receptionist would say, "Sir, you just came yesterday."

"I know, but I really need to get a job here."

I don't know if I would have lasted longer than at the other two factories, but at the time it was the job to get because you would be set for life. That being said, I am so glad they never called me back. It was good work, with a good retirement plan, but I would have worked there for thirty-five years and never have made it to where I am today.

Instead, I kept training to become a professional wrestler. And I was learning the business. Sylvio Samson had me help him promote shows on Saturdays; we put posters in every shop window in the city. Sometimes shop owners wanted tickets in exchange, but most of the time they let us do it for free. The first time I saw my name on one of those posters, it got me really excited about my future: *Combat préliminaire: Pat Patterson vs. Cyclone Samson.*

I always told my family when I was competing, but they never came to see me. I wished they had been there just like they were when my brother was playing hockey. The first time my parents saw me in the ring was many years later in San Francisco. It was quite the shock for them as I picked them up in a Cadillac and brought them to my big house. My mother kept crying in the car because she had never before even sat in a Caddie. And she could not believe my place was actually my house. I was headlining the Cow Palace, the Montréal Forum of San Francisco, at the time . . . But there I go again, getting ahead of myself.

My dad and I kept arguing about me getting a real job. Men didn't show affection back then, not even fathers and sons. I had nothing in common with him anyway. We never found anything to bond over on any level. The reality was the family was just too big and everyone just wanted to get the hell out as soon as possible. Everyone was always invading everyone else's space when we were together at home. Dad was strict and I hated all the rules. And I was always looking for affection — that was not his strong point.

The reality, too, was that on a personal level I still really didn't know who I was. I'd tried going dancing with girls like any other boy, but I knew almost from the start that it wasn't for me. I never knew why, but girls just weren't doing it for me, even if I found them cute. I had a friend in my class who was gay. At the time, he knew where the gay tavern was, so we started going there Friday nights. When the waiter spotted us, he told us we were too young, but then he told us to be quiet and sit in the corner. I don't know why he didn't kick us out, maybe because he wanted to help. It was quite the sight — everyone in there was cruising me. I was a good-looking young man. After going a few times, I finally met a guy my age — I must've been sixteen, closer to seventeen — at this tavern. As they say, he was very good-looking, too. We started talking and one thing led to another.

He brought me to his place because his parents were out of town. It was incredible, and I felt so good afterward. There was tenderness and affection. We were just two people, together, sharing their feelings. It was a strange sentiment. In fact, I couldn't think straight anymore.

I got back home around 1 a.m.; I had missed my curfew, so every door was locked and I had to ring the doorbell to get in. I knew I would wake up everybody but I didn't care. My dad was doubly pissed — because I wasn't home on time and now I'd woken him up — and my mom tried to play peacemaker. While I wasn't completely drunk, I was still floating on the alcohol I'd had plus the incredible evening I'd experienced. That's when, with the alcohol helping me muster my courage, I completely opened up.

"I need to tell you something: I think I'm in love."

My mother was happy for me, telling me how good that was. Then I added that it was another boy who made me feel this way. More than likely it was the buzz speaking for me, but I felt too good to keep it a secret.

My dad was like, "*Quoi?*" *What?* "Don't tell me you have become a *tapette?*"

I defended myself the best I could. "I'm not a *tapette.*"

"I won't have a *tapette* in my home; you're going to have to move out."

My mother started to cry. "Gérard, you can't do that to our son."

He snapped: "I can't have a *tapette* in my house. What will everyone say?"

This was the turning point. I'd wanted to leave home for the circus but hadn't had the guts. I knew I had to get the hell out and the sooner the better. My mom ended up winning that argument and I was allowed to stay a little longer, but I had learned that Dad was not ready to share this with me. Things would get smoother as the years went by, but I was in New York before we truly spoke about that night again.

I was working at the shoe factory around that time and I gave all the money I made to my mother. She would give me back a little money, and with that I would go to the tavern. I had found a place where I could be myself, where people understood me, where we would talk until closing time.

Fast-forward a few years to the end of 1960: I was still working for Samson outside the city. The Boston promoter Tony Santos came to Montréal to check out the talent and he brought some people to his territory. One night, I got hold of him on his way out of the matches at Paul Sauvé Arena, on the corner of Beaubien and Pie-IX.

"Me. Talk to you. Want to wrestle for you in Boston. Give me start."

To which he answered, "Argh, take my card!"

When I think about it now, he was trying to blow me off, but I took that as a *yes*. There was no stopping me; my mind was made up. I found an old suitcase in the garbage and put everything I owned in there. My mom could not believe I was leaving, but I was. When I finally left, my dad told me he didn't want me coming back, knocking on his door ever again, and I never did. I promised myself not to. Strangely, that made him mad, even though he was the one who said it in the first place.

I wished I could have spared my mom from all the shit she went through when I left home. I borrowed twenty bucks (a lot of money at the time) from my sister Claudette and left for Boston on a Greyhound bus. I was nineteen years old, had no plan, and barely any money. What was I thinking? I guess it's a good thing I *wasn't* thinking too much, because today I'm glad I left. Little did I know, I was going to meet my soul mate and embark upon a career that, more than fifty years later, I still love.

Boston here I come, with my suitcase straight out of a garbage can.

BOSTON, MY LOVE

"I've loved, I've laughed and cried"

In the early 1960s, everything was so much easier. Immigration to the United States was not a big problem. The big problem was that my English was limited. Actually, it was terrible.

At the border, all I had was that business card and a letter from a wrestling promoter, and I attempted to explain that I was going to work for this man Tony Santos in Boston. Three hours later, customs was finally able to get in touch with him, and he said I was coming to wrestle for him. I was lucky he said so. Once they had that confirmation, I was allowed to enter the country and work here. Imagine trying that today!

I was dropped at the Greyhound bus stop in Boston with my five-word English vocabulary and barely any money left in my pocket. There was a little man called Bobo who was waiting for me there — he was a wrestler, too. I was three hours late, but he was there waiting for me as per Santos's request.

This guy told me we were going to walk to the apartment complex where all the wrestlers stayed. It still stands there today

In a Boston restaurant like this I would slowly learn English.

at 72 Westland Avenue, right around the corner from the Boston Symphony Hall on Massachusetts Avenue. I was tired and wished we could take a cab, but neither of us had any money, so we walked. It was an incredibly long walk, close to an hour. Thank God I had a lot of practice from Montréal.

When we arrived, I was introduced to the landlord, Ralph, whom I proceeded to torture mercilessly with my pranks for the next year or so. It was a six-floor building, with maybe three to five rooms on each side of a giant staircase and a shared bathroom. It cost ten dollars a week for a room furnished with a bed, a table, and a small black-and-white television. Some of the other non-wrestling tenants were old people who would pass out drunk on the stairs on a regular basis. It was quite the place — not exactly the Ritz. (Today that property is probably worth millions.) Still I had fun. We all talked to each other from room to room. It was a big change from my family's place in Montréal: I didn't share my space with ten other people. Living all by myself, I felt like I was on top of the world. I even had hot water. All in all, it was a big improvement for me.

I had so much fun living in that place, enjoying my new life and freedom while playing pranks on the people who had the misfortune of renting a room near me.

My English was, as I've said, terrible. I made all the classic mistakes French people make when learning English. We just take the French word and try to say it in English. So I would say *gouvernement* instead of government, only I added an English pronunciation. I probably don't have to tell you, but everyone was always laughing at my attempts to speak English. But living with so many different people helped. They asked me often enough to repeat myself. The more I talked to people, the more functional English I learned. What really helped was television, especially *The Price Is Right*. I learned the best I could like that, so if you don't like my English, blame TV.

My first week in Boston, I ate the same thing every day: hamburger steak. Why? Simply because I had no idea what anything else on the menu was. One time, the special was pork chops and I knew I liked *chop de porc frais*, so I was about to try it because the names were so similar. When they asked me if I wanted "gravy," I was sure I was not going to like the meal.

"Just hamburger steak," I said.

My friend ordered the pork chops with gravy. When I saw what they brought him, I knew I would be ordering it soon.

And so I added "pork chop" and a few more words along my way and started to expand my knowledge of English.

When it came time to wrestle, I had no problem. I had learned enough wrestling lingo in Montréal to keep up in any ring. They had a gym with a nice ring at the wrestling office, located in the old Boston arena on St. Botolph, now the Matthews Arena, a ten-minute walk from my place. They even kept the wrestling bear there. I wrestled it once and that was enough for me — it was much scarier than any human opponent. On my first day at the office, I met Golden Boy Dupree. He was thirty-five and gay, as I later found out. Santos wanted me to wrestle with him, so he could see how good I was. I passed that test with flying colors: Golden Boy was very happy and Santos told me not to worry, that I was booked. Three or four days later, he drove Golden Boy and me to wrestle on a show in Buffalo. It's a seven-hour drive from Boston to Buffalo. In Montréal, I did a few long trips but never one that long. Since my English was so shitty, I had no idea I was in for such a long ride and the conversation was almost nonexistent.

We got there early and Santos bought us each a sandwich. We were going to wrestle in the opening match even though no one knew who we were. That night, I walked into the ring in front of 6,000 people. It was impressive for someone like me; I'd only wrestled in front of much smaller crowds. We had a very good match — even though we were nervous — and the local promoter and Santos were happy. We went back to Boston right after the show. A few days later, Santos brought me a check for fifty dollars. Fifty dollars for one match? I was rich! Then Santos laid it out on me. "You have to pay

Earliest wrestling picture on record. I look good, don't I!

me transportation." So he took thirty-five dollars for himself and left me with fifteen. I had never owned a car or bought gas, so I had no idea how paying "trans" worked. He was screwing me, but I didn't know that at the time. Later, when I was in Oregon, the wrestlers had a proper system where you paid between two and five cents per mile to the car owner.

Santos was quite the character, even for a promoter, and he used all sorts of names for his wrestlers — like Bruno Sa*n*martino instead of Bruno Sa*m*martino. Before the internet, something that simple was often enough to confuse fans into coming, thinking that the big star would be there. But it was always some sort of cheap copy played by an unknown.

After Buffalo, all we ever did was wrestle in small buildings around Boston for no real money. Santos's son, Tony Jr., brought the ring from show to show and I traveled with him and helped set it up. I was on the ring crew all the time.

When I wasn't wrestling I was enjoying life in a new city with new friends who were young like me; we talked and dreamt together about what our lives would be like. I didn't explore Boston much, because I didn't want to get lost. I mostly stayed in the Fenway neighborhood. All in all, not a bad place to discover the world.

I got comfortable living in my building and began to have some fun at the expense of everyone there. Every Sunday morning we would all go downstairs one after the other and see the old man to pay the rent. Poor Ralph. He was quite the sight, always in a bathrobe. He had a dog named Jippy who followed him everywhere. I was doing OK, but I didn't have much money for anything fancy like curtains for my windows. Ralph had beautiful curtains in his place, so one day, I told one of the guys to tell Ralph he was charging them too much.

That made Ralph mad. "If you don't like it, then get out!" Ralph yelled and got all worked up just like I wanted.

While that was going on, I jumped on a chair, stole his curtains, and brought them up to my room. He never suspected me. For some mysterious reason, Ralph always liked me. He would curse everybody else, especially the drunken tenants, but he was always nice to me. I can't believe how much I abused his faith.

Cooking in my small apartment in Boston.
I have good memories from that place!

There was one tenant, a Japanese man, who never closed the door of his apartment when he went to the shared bathroom. So I would lock him out of his apartment, and he'd have to yell for Ralph to come up and let him in.

Another time, I let the water run in the bathtub all night in the second-floor bathroom. Next morning, Ralph called out to me, "Patterson, there is some serious shit going on around here!"

"What do you mean, Ralph?" I answered as if I was still half-asleep, playing dumb.

"Let me show you."

He brought me over to his apartment. Water was dripping down the wall from the ceiling. It was goddamn Niagara Falls in there.

"Patterson, you're going to help me find out who's responsible for that shit."

Then he brought me to the basement where there was a barber-shop and there was water dripping everywhere. I started to get very nervous and hoped he would never find out I was the culprit. Thank God, he trusted me. I didn't intend to cause damage like that, I just thought it would be funny. I was dumb, but I never did anything in my life that was mean-spirited; I just wanted to make people laugh and entertain myself with their laughter. Unfortunately for Ralph, I was just getting started.

One time, we all took our feather-filled pillows and made the biggest indoor snowstorm of all time. The following day, there was Ralph trying to clean up our mess. He was almost done and there was a humongous pile of feathers in the middle of the lobby. Out of nowhere, I yelled, "Ralph, what's up this morning?" and then I started to run downstairs.

He yelled back, in hopes of stopping me, "Don't go out the door. Please!"

But I ignored him, opened the door, and in came the wind. The feathers went flying everywhere all over again! It was funny as hell for everyone — except for poor Ralph.

One night, Ralph knocked on my door and told me everyone was complaining about the music coming from my apartment.

"It's not that loud and it's only 10 p.m. I'm just playing the radio. Come on, Ralph. Let's have a beer!"

"I don't drink beer," he lied.

"Come on, would one beer kill you?"

So he comes in with his dog and sits down with me and my friend. We're drinking beer and we're telling all kind of stories. Then he takes a second beer. I was home free. By the third beer, he's feeling real good. Suddenly he stands up and starts to look around my place, and he goes, "Where did you get those drapes?"

I was so busted. But I decided to plead complete innocence. "They were there when I took the place, Ralph. What do you mean?"

The Japanese guy saved the day by knocking on my door to complain that the music was still too loud. Ralph took his anger out on him and told him to go to hell, and he came back to party with us. Later, he got hot again about the curtains and said to his dog, "Jippy, let's get out. This is no place for a gentleman."

At some point, a fire alarm was installed in the building. And, of course, almost every night like clockwork, someone would pull the alarm . . . OK, it was almost always me, but everyone was laughing as we ran outside half-naked. Those were the crazy days. When you don't know anything, you don't worry about anything. I didn't know you could get arrested pulling those kinds of pranks. I was lucky I never got into any real trouble.

There were no phones in our rooms, so we went across the street to a phone booth to make calls. Ralph had a phone in the lobby, however, so one time I put shoe polish on the earpiece and then phoned from across the street. I disguised my voice and said the call was for Haystack *Muldoon*. Santos used Muldoon to confuse fans into thinking he was Haystacks Calhoun. Poor overweight Muldoon had to come downstairs from his top-floor apartment to answer the phone. I kept him on the line for a few seconds then hung up. When I re-entered the building, Ralph and Muldoon were both upset and had an ear that was shoe-polish black. I burst out laughing again.

Ralph, you've been gone for a long time, but I just want to say I'm sorry. You had me laughing like crazy half the time I lived there. I still laugh when I think about you. Thank you.

While all of this was going on, I worked for Santos as much as I could, mostly small shows. Finally, he collaborated with another promoter to put on a big show at the Boston Garden on April 4, 1961. All of my wrestling gear back then was purple like my idol Kowalski's. And who was in the main event that night? Kowalski! He lived in Boston for years, so it was only natural. I was in the same dressing room with him for the first time. My heart was racing very fast. I overheard Santos say to him, "Watch the kid work: he wrestles just like you."

I wrestled second or third, and Kowalski took the time to watch my match. Afterwards, he said, "You did all right, kid." I was happy as shit. I asked if he remembered signing my picture at the Montréal Forum, and I was overjoyed when he said, "I remember." Kowalski was a good guy, who never drank and always wanted to help the younger wrestlers.

The Garden, just like Buffalo, turned into a one- or two-shot deal. But Santos took care of me and I often traveled with him. I was learning in the ring, gaining more experience but not learning much about the business side of wrestling. I was still naive with limited

English, but my reputation as a wrestler was growing.

I wrestled with everyone who was anyone in Boston — Frankie Scarpa (who was also known as Manuel Cortez), Bull Montana, and Bull Curry. Everyone wanted to wrestle with the kid in the purple trunks, because I would take crazy bumps for them. Bull Curry was quite the character, and definitely not pretty. He was known for two things: being crazy and being cheap. My first night in, he bought me a beer. I remember telling myself I must have made an impression.

Boston wasn't as wild as San Francisco was a few years later, but playing the bad guy still meant you might have to fend off an attack by fans. One night, a guy jumped in the ring and tried to strangle me with a rope. "Killer" Pat Patterson was about to get killed . . . Thank God I made it out alive. Other fans loved me. In Worcester, not far from Boston, a girl named Marika Niedzial started my fan club. Every week, I would see her at the shows. She would send fan club members the pictures she took of me by mail. She brought me gifts and all sort of things. I was freaking out: *there was a Pat Patterson fan club.* It was so strange for me to get all that attention just for doing something I loved.

One time, Santos brought in "the girls" to wrestle the entire loop as an attraction. One of them was future WWE Hall of Famer Mae Young. Santos wanted me to ride with her, so she would know how to get to our shows. (Remember, there was no such thing as GPS in my day.) She showed up in a brand-new car, looking like a movie star, and she said, "Patterson, get in the car" while smoking the biggest cigar I had ever seen. She asked if I ever smoked and when I said no, she said, "If you want to be a top guy, you might as well start. Light it up for me."

Then I saw her wrestle. Holy shit! I told myself that I never wanted-ed to get in there with her. It was a tag team match, and she was really beating the hell out of those girls. She looked like a star. After the match, she had me drinking beer after telling me I needed to do that too if I wanted to be a star.

Let's just say, she was a little rough around the edges. I would see her once in a while when she was in town and for a while she lived across the street from me. She even came by my apartment just to shoot the crap like one of the boys. By then, I had rented a slightly bigger place in the same building that included a little kitchenette, a bedroom, and a small living room for five dollars extra a month.

One night around 1 a.m., I heard banging on my door. It was Mae Young wearing only her bra and panties with a martini in her hand. What the hell?

"Patterson, let me in."

"What's the matter?"

"Don't worry, Pat, I just want to talk bullshit with you."

She kept on talking forever that night, telling me how good I was and how far I would go in the business. She finally passed out, so I put her in my bed and slept on the floor.

The next morning, I had to help her get home since she was still in rough shape. When I got home, I realized she had pissed all over my bed. I don't remember if I gave her clothes or if she left in the morning as half-naked as she had come in the night before. Still I never let her forget that she left that surprise in my bed. I loved her dearly.

As you can guess, I was still not into women. I hadn't known how I'd live my personal life among new guys in a new city when I'd come to Boston. But being gay turned out to not be an issue at all. As long as I took five- and ten-dollar wrestling payoffs without complaining, the promoter couldn't have cared less. There were even a few other wrestlers who were gay. I was lucky everyone liked me and I was accepted right away for who I was.

One night sometime in the middle of all my early Boston experiences, Golden Boy brought me to a bar. And that's where I met

Louie Dondero for the first time. We kept staring at each other all evening. I remember he looked spectacular but I didn't dare speak to him because he was with another man named Lee. The next day, I asked Golden Boy to set me up on a date with Louie. And who arrived? Lee!

I said to myself, "What the hell! He's not the one I wanted." Lee was all over me because he thought I was interested in him. We only had a couple of drinks and I told him I was sorry but it wasn't going anywhere.

The next day, I asked Golden Boy why he had set me up with the guy.

"You asked for Lee, didn't you?"

"I meant L-O-U-I-E."

I told you my English was really bad.

Golden Boy called Louie this time and set me up.

Louie picked me up in his brand-new Buick. I was impressed right away. A young guy driving a car like that was unusual. And did I mention he looked spectacular?

We got drinks and we got quite a bit cozier than I'd been on my previous date. At that very moment, who came in the bar? Of course, it was Lee. It turned into a little argument, but Louie wasn't bothered by it. We started to see a lot of each other.

Louie came to see me every weekend and each Wednesday on his Harley-Davidson. He lived in Leominster, near Boston, and he worked in a slaughterhouse, killing chickens and earning good money. When I had time off, I would hang out with him or go to work with him. I would stay at his mom and dad's place. They were Italian, and I discovered Italian food with them. I knew nothing about the world when I lived in Montréal; in Boston, I was getting my first real taste of it. Louie's father was a chef and he introduced me to all kinds of delicious food. He made an incredibly tasty salad with everything in it — I was used to eating salad with just lettuce and some vinegar. I had never had so many good things in my life.

As open-minded as his parents were, we still kept up the façade of just being friends. We didn't open up about our relationship until years later when we brought them to visit in San Francisco. Louie has been gone for more than fifteen years now and I am still close with his brothers and his sister, as well as our nieces and nephews. They are my family. But all of this is for another chapter.

Around this time, I got myself booked for three weeks in Montréal. I wanted to introduce my friend to *my* family, especially to my mother. We drove up in Louie's brand-new car, so I wasn't coming home with a bum. I was really proud of him. Even today, it's difficult to write exactly how I felt about him. Bear with me — I will try to figure this out as we continue along this journey. I have just now realized how deep the camouflage of who we were extends. Can I truly ever be free to be who I really am?

Louie didn't spoke a word of French and my family didn't know any English. Everyone made the best of it, and I translated things as needed. The whole family fell in love with Louie. He was such a great person. To this day, one of my sisters keeps a photograph of him, and when she needs guidance, she looks at it. "He helps me a lot," she tells me all the time. I'm not sure I understand, but it makes me happy.

Louie had that kind of long-lasting effect on everyone he met. It was good to be accepted, but it was always under the pretense that he was only my friend. We never introduced ourselves as in a relationship or showed affection in public. We were hiding in plain sight. Our unofficial cover for years was always: "He's just a friend." *Friend* is still the only way I feel comfortable describing him even though we were so much more. That just goes to show you how deep you needed to pretend back in the day. Even if things have changed since, that is one habit I still can't completely shake off.

Unless we were with our gay friends, like some of the wrestlers in Boston, we were in the proverbial closet. For work, I was in a double bind: I had to protect my personal home life and I had to protect the business. I was in two closets.

After returning to Boston, I got a letter from Maurice "Mad Dog" Vachon. He'd seen me wrestle and was impressed with how good I was becoming. In fact, he thought

Louie and I were young, carefree, and in love. We looked good, too!

so much of me that he wanted me to go to Oregon to work for Don Owen, one of the most well-respected promoters at the time.

Maurice's letter said I was booked in Portland in two weeks and that he was waiting for me. I was speechless. He wasn't asking me if I was interested, he was giving me a starting date! Remember, this was very different era — all Don Owen knew about me was what Maurice had told him. I was dumbfounded, realizing the scope of Mad Dog's confidence in my abilities.

When Santos learned about the offer, he got me into his office right away for a big spectacle, designed to scare me into staying in Boston. He had the biggest desk I had ever seen, bigger than a kitchen table. He proceeded to unfold in front of me the biggest map in the world, at least that's how I felt seeing such a thing for the first time. It was so big I was sure that the unfolding would never end. He showed me the distance between Boston and Portland and told me, "It's coast to coast, kid. You're going around the world. Atlantic Ocean to the Pacific Ocean. Are you ready for this?"

I knew nothing and I really thought I would be traveling around the world to get there. I was scared shitless. I didn't have a car. Jeez, I didn't even know how to drive. And I had no money, since I was barely making fifteen dollars a night in Boston.

"Me no go," I told him.

When I didn't show up in Portland, Maurice sent me a second letter, giving me hell and shit because I no-showed and he had put his word on the line for me. He also gave me a second starting date, warning me that I better make it or he was going to beat the crap out of me next time he saw me. My situation in Boston hadn't improved in between letters. For all I knew, wrestling in Boston was taking me nowhere and fast. So, I got a loan from Louie and bought a plane ticket to take the first flight of my life — to Portland.

Before that big trip, I decided to visit my family in Montréal once again. I went with Louie for three weeks; I didn't know when I would be able to return. On our way back from that visit, we had a big car accident in middle-of-nowhere Vermont. It's the scariest thing that has ever happened to me on the road, even though I logged miles and miles in the years to come. I don't know how we survived it. That there were no consequences, not even scratches or bruises, was a miracle. We weren't even wearing seat belts, can you believe that?

The car rolled over three times and was upside down in a ditch when we finally came to rest. We had to kick the door open and crawl out in the snow and mud. It was probably around six in the morning, the middle of winter, and pitch black. There was nothing around as far as we could see. We had to walk a long goddamn way before finding a house to use their phone. We were able to notify the police and call Louie's family to come and pick us up.

Once we got back to their place, Louie's father, who had been drinking, was mad at me for wrecking the car. The old man jumped me out of nowhere and we started to fight. He was so mad. I remember it like it was yesterday, him yelling, "You tried to kill my son!"

It was not a pretty sight.

I was confused beyond belief. *Louie was driving.* It was *his car.* What the hell? I understand better now how scared he must have been, but still, if I said my feelings were not hurt, I would be lying. The worst part was that there was no fixing it; I didn't have time. I was

Louie came to see me off to Portland and even helped me pay for my first plane ticket.

leaving Louie to deal with the fallout of the accident all by himself. Portland and Mad Dog were waiting for me, and I couldn't miss that second opportunity. And to be honest, the wrath of Maurice "Mad Dog" Vachon scared me more than Louie's father.

In a sense, I was relieved that my relationship with Louie was being put on hold. We were getting really close, but I was afraid of my feelings for him. I didn't want a relationship to hold me back as I tried to carve out a career for myself in wrestling.

What I didn't know yet is that true love can conquer anything, even distance. As my career was about to take off, that man would literally follow me to the other end of the known world — or at least it seemed like it was for us.

PORTLAND AND
EVERYTHING IN-BETWEEN

"I traveled each and every highway"

Moving to Oregon was a big step. I was still that little kid from Mon-tréal barely able to speak the language. It was scary. Luckily for me, it worked out.

I am not the first to say it and I won't be the last, but it needs to be said: Don Owen was a great person first, and a great promoter second. It was my first time traveling a regular circuit in a territory and building up matches on television. On my first night in Portland, I was in the opener and I had a good match. Afterward I got my envelope and he had paid me $300! I went to Maurice and told him that there must have been a mistake, that it was too much. Mad Dog told me with his legendary voice, "Don't worry, you are still getting screwed!" And then he burst out laughing. I had never made so much money doing what I love.

That kind of big payoff only happened once a month; most of the time we wrestled in armories where the dressing rooms didn't even have showers. It was important to shower after a match in those days: the mats were dirty and you could get a staph infection easily. We had to go to the bathroom to shower, where fans went to relieve themselves. It was almost as if I was back living in Montreal!

Speaking of dressing rooms, there's something I need to get off my chest. The Michael Sam thing bugs me because journalists assume dressing rooms are anti-gay. That kid played football all of his life. It wouldn't be any different in the NFL. It's the same in wrestling. In my day, we had to shower together and scratch each other's back and it was never an issue. Not once did one of my colleagues refuse to work a match with me because I was gay. Strangely enough, of all places, Michael Sam ended up playing pro in my hometown, with the Montréal Alouettes of the CFL.

Don Owen was a man of his word and we were always paid what he promised, to the exact dime every time. I appeared in a few main events, and the money became very nice, something like $300 a week on average. After living off seventy a week in Boston, it was a big improvement. And the Portland promotion was a fun territory with short trips. We would go to Seattle, Washington, and return to Oregon that same night. I was still growing as a performer, competing against some big stars including former National Wrestling Alliance world champion Pat O'Connor. Now, that was a learning experience.

O'Connor always wanted to lead and he always wanted to wrestle like he was fighting for his life. One day, I finally mustered up the courage to ask, "Can I speak with you, sir, without you getting mad?"

"Sure, kid. What's up?"

"What is it you don't like wrestling with me?"

"No, I love wrestling with you."

I had my opening so I explained to him how we could have much better matches. I wanted him to let me do my thing as the villain so that he, the hero, could shine. "Let's go out there and tear the house down," I told him.

He said he would think about it, and when he finally let me lead in a match, it was like night and day. Another thing: Pat was the cheapest wrestler I had met yet. He didn't spend a penny, not on anything. After that good match we had, he bought me a beer at the bar. I almost had a heart attack.

Everyone has to be produced: whether you're Pat O'Connor, Ric Flair, John Cena, Frank Sinatra, or even Michael Jackson. After a while, stars get into a habit and the show becomes stale because they only want to do their usual thing. The worst part is, in many cases, no one around them wants to tell them. The magic of what we do in a wrestling ring follows the same principle as in a good movie when the hero is down. That desperation needs to register with the audience. They have to believe he needs their support to come back. People have to identify with you. I already knew a lot about what works in the ring by that point, and I consider myself very lucky to have learned from so many more great teachers in the years to come. But if anyone had told me *I* would be the teacher one day, I would never have believed them.

In Portland, I was Maurice's boy and Maurice was the top star, so I was golden with Don Owen. Don took very good care of me, but he still asked me for favors. "Talk to Maurice. He's creating way too much trouble with his shit. We are going to have problems."

I would go to Maurice and ask him to tone things down. He would shout back in French, "*Qui mange de la merde le colisse!*" There is no perfect translation for that bit of colorful French lingo . . . Let us just say that Mad Dog said something about eating shit and leave it at that. Really, Maurice was so over, he could get away with almost anything. One night, I saw him wrestle Luther Lindsay in a sixty-minute match. I had never seen anything like it. Ten minutes from the end, everyone in the armory was standing on their feet. I told myself one day I would create the same reaction.

I'd moved to Oregon without Louie, and as far as I was concerned, we'd split up. But I'd never told Louie that quite so bluntly. He had a job, a very good job, and I never expected he'd leave it behind. And, to be completely honest, I didn't want him to come with me.

Before I left Boston, he'd asked me, "When will I see you again?"

"I don't know, Louie; we might meet again. I will go there for a while and we'll see."

What was I going to do with him? I was moving to the other side of the country, and I didn't want to bring him out there to face it — it was 1962, what kind of reception would we get? My career always came first, end of discussion. Louie understood the choice I was making. He knew how important wrestling was to me. He was, without a doubt, beyond my mother, the first person who completely understood and accepted me inside and out.

I had been in Portland for a month and a half when I realized I needed Louie in my life. We had been writing to each other and one day I wrote to him to come to Portland because I was just missing him too much. He left his job and his family to be with me. If that's not pure and unadulterated love, I don't know what is. I never regretted my decision to ask him to come and join me in Portland. I would have gotten myself in trouble for sure without him. I'm a lucky man.

We stayed at my hotel for a couple of weeks as we looked for an apartment of our own. At first, I was hiding him and that wasn't fun. One night, Mad Dog Vachon showed up in the hotel lobby a little drunk. Louie was afraid of Mad Dog and he took off, as if he had just seen the devil himself. I can't really blame him because we were all scared of the Dog at one point or another. Maurice knew I was gay. He had met Louie when I came back from Boston to wrestle in Montréal and naturally he had figured things out. Seeing Louie in Portland, Mad Dog got himself all worked up. He had vouched for me and now I was putting him in a precarious position. "You prick, you double-crossed me . . . You brought your boyfriend here . . ."

"Maurice, he's my friend," I said, "and he's important to me."

"Where is he?" Mad Dog yelled, madder than ever.

"I don't know. When he saw you, he bolted."

"We'll find him," he said.

We jumped in his car and we drove around downtown, Maurice getting madder by the minute. It was no fun for me at all. We had been driving for over half an hour when I finally spotted Louie. Mad Dog stepped on the gas, we stopped right beside him, and Mad Dog growled, "Get in the car!"

Louie started running for his life as if he'd just been sentenced to death.

"The bastard, I will get him."

Maurice stepped on it again and he actually got on the goddamn sidewalk to block Louie from escaping.

I tried to calm everyone down and salvage the situation. "Louie, please, get in the car."

He reluctantly got in the backseat. And that's when Maurice said, "We go to the hotel and we drink."

Louie didn't drink much more than a beer usually. Mad Dog wanted us to drink scotch. I figured he was getting ready to kill both of us, so we drank. He started a conversation with Louie, and they didn't stop talking all night. They became good friends. I could not believe it. Throughout his life, Maurice had never been afraid to open his mind to new things. I guess he figured out that Louie and I were great people who just happened to be gay. In the years to come, the same thing happened with a lot of people who had never known anyone gay before.

I'd had a comparable experience moving to Portland. In Montréal, there were almost no black people in my neighborhood. In Portland, Shag Thomas, a former football player, was one of the star wrestlers. He was the first black person I became friends with. He had a wonderful family and one night he invited Mad Dog and me to visit. It was quite an experience for me — the first time I went to a house where everyone was black. I was discovering the world all right, and appreciated meeting all kinds of different people. That probably doesn't seem noteworthy today, but to me, as a gay man, it was uplifting to see that we could all get along and love each other with all of our differences.

Now that I think of it, Maurice Vachon was instrumental in helping people in the business accept Louie and me. Maurice was so well respected in Portland, and since I was teaming with him, no one bothered me; the other wrestlers were even encouraging me. Whenever we traveled, Maurice would ask, "Where's Louie?"

And when I'd say, "Well, he stayed home, Maurice," Mad Dog would shake his head.

"*Tabarnak*, why does he stay there all alone? He doesn't know anyone."

"I can't bring him to wrestling."

"He's my buddy, we bring him with us."

So, I told Louie that Maurice wanted him to come on trips with us. I wasn't going to argue with Mad Dog, and neither was Louie. We both knew better. Everywhere we went, Maurice introduced Louie as *his* friend. Louie got over right away with everyone, first because of Mad Dog and then because he made friends easily.

I became good friends with Nick Bockwinkel around that time as well. He went on to win the AWA Championship and our paths crossed many times. One day, Nick said that his wife, Darlene, wanted to meet Louie and he invited us for dinner at their place. I don't

Louie briefly became an on-and-off character in my act.

remember how exactly Nick had come to know of Louie and my relationship, just that it wasn't a big deal to him. Darlene really hit it off with Louie and they became great pals. We had them over for dinner at our place. They loved Louie so much, they started to talk about him with everyone they met. They were putting us over like crazy. "Pat's friend, Louie, he's such a great guy and what a chef."

All the wrestlers wanted to meet him. "Pat, when are we getting an invitation to eat at your place?" Wrestlers love to hang around with each other and we never say no to a free meal. When I started to move from territory to territory, Louie's reputation was always stellar, and I can thank Maurice and Nick for that. I bet you didn't expect that from a bunch of wrestlers in the 1960s.

It is surprising that in the world of wrestling, where you might expect all those macho guys to be homophobic, that it was never an issue — at least not in my case. A friend of mine recently told me that if Michael Jordan had been gay, it would not have mattered because he was so good and drew so many people to his sport, that no one would have said anything bad about him. The same thing applied to me, according to my friend — I was special and that's why I was accepted. Special? I don't know. I don't think I should be compared to Michael Jordan; I just think it's important to stress how easy it was for me to gain acceptance. Then again, I was never openly gay in front of the wrestlers. I never talked about it in the dressing room. I was always joking and being one of the guys, so unless you were close to me, you never truly knew.

I was no angel, though. I liked to have fun and party like any guy. But I was gay, and I had to be careful about showing who I really was. I couldn't draw attention by flirting with men at the hotel bar or bringing guys back to my room. I couldn't tell the other wrestlers stories about my conquests the way that most guys were bragging about how many girls they slept with that week or how many honeys were waiting for them in their hotel room. Some of the wrestlers even used me as an alibi with their wives. They knew their wives would feel secure if they believed their husbands were with me. I would say hello to the wife on the phone, helping to ensure I was part of the boys even though I never allowed myself to be myself around them.

Half the time, I protected wrestling against all the naysayers and the other half, I spent it hiding my personal life from my colleagues so that they would feel more comfortable around me. Maybe that's why I never met another gay couple in wrestling. There were those wrestlers in Boston who were gay, but they were never part of a couple. If there were gay wrestlers around me in Portland, I just didn't know then. Maybe they just didn't feel comfortable to share their life with me, just like I didn't share mine with the boys. As a gay wrestler, I was living in not just one but two closets. (I know I've already written that — but if you want the complete Pat Patterson experience, some stories and ideas will repeat themselves. That's how it goes.)

Louie appreciated what Maurice did for us and they remained good friends throughout the years. Much later, when we were living in Florida and had a beautiful home on the canal, we had not seen Maurice in years. Mad Dog was not rich, and he was at the tail end of his career. He let us know that he would love to visit us if he could. Without hesitation, Louie said, "Just tell me when; bring your wife and some friends." I think Maurice stayed for a month and Louie took real good care of him.

Vince McMahon and Mad Dog only met one-on-one a couple of times. But I have told Vince so many stories about him that he fell in love with him and his character. I was damn proud, and thankful to Vince, to have been able to repay Mad Dog a little for all he did for Louie and me by helping to get him inducted into the WWE Hall of Fame in 2010. It was something he deserved.

Just before we went on stage the night of the ceremony, Mad Dog asked me how much he was being paid.

"Five hundred," I said.

"What! Only five hundred?"

"No, Maurice, I'm just kidding — it's five thousand."

He kept repeating the number, as he could not believe he was making that much money for so little work. We had a good laugh. It was the last time we saw each other. There is no doubt in my mind that without him I would not be here writing this book. When he passed away in 2013, I was sad because he had been so strong when I first met him, I felt that this man would live forever. But we all meet our maker, no matter what. Friends of mine, who had access to his picture collection after he was gone, told me that one of the few wrestling photos not of Maurice or his family was one of Louie and me in Portland. Maurice will have a special place in my heart forever as well.

There were gay bars in Oregon; they were not as out in the open as in Montréal, but we got by. I would wrestle and Louie would stay home in our little apartment. He took care of our place and cooked food. Sometimes, I would be gone for a week in Seattle for a bigger tour.

Louie had lived all of his life in the same city with his family, who he was close with. He had never been anywhere until we started living together and moving for my work. Louie made friends very quickly wherever we went, because everyone loved him, and I think he enjoyed the adventure as much as I did. He was two years older than me and a little wiser. Whenever we moved to a different place in the same city, Louie hunted for a new apartment and made a first visit. When I was available and back from the road, we would go see it together. He was great. The "friend" of my dreams, I was lucky to have found the person who wanted to share my life with me. We were perfect for each other. Still, my career was very important to me, and in the Portland years I was looking for a way that Louie might become a part of it.

Harry Elliott was the promoter in Seattle, Washington, who worked for Don Owen. He came up to me one day saying that he had a great idea, that he was going to do something good with me. He knew that I had a "friend," so he came up with the character "Pretty Boy" Pat Patterson. I would wear lipstick, use a long cigarette holder, and wear sunglasses and a beret. Louie made me a flamboyant ring jacket and he would also play the role of my chauffeur/manager. We had that kind of stereotypical abusive wrestler–manager/valet relationship where I'd push him around when he dropped something and generally make his life miserable. It was done to make people hate me and feel sorry for him — a little bit like the Ted DiBiase and Virgil relationship years later in WWE for those of you familiar with that story.

One night I was wrestling a Japanese wrestler named Haru Sasaki, who was really popular. I sent him outside the ring and he got at Louie, chopping and kicking him. I went completely crazy, selling how mad and distressed I was that Louie was being mistreated *by someone else.* I then defended my poor manservant and beat the other wrestler for attacking my property. People felt even sorrier for Louie. Louie loved being a manager. I wasn't too much into it, but it worked for a while. When I would rough him up as part of the show, I would get so much reaction from the fans.

The "Pretty Boy" gimmick was only used in Seattle at first. (The television broadcast of the show from Portland didn't reach Seattle, and vice versa, even though it was the same territory.) Don Owen didn't like the angle. But when he kept hearing stories about how the thing was getting over, one night he said, "Why don't you wear the goddamn beret and the gimmick and everything?"

To be completely honest, I was embarrassed doing that at first because it's not me in real life. But even while doing that gimmick, I never had problems with the other wrestlers. I was so good that everyone wanted to work with me, whatever their feelings might have been about my personal life. Some of the old-timers who always stayed in the same territory knew I would extend their careers. If anyone had a problem with me and who I was, it was never brought up.

Despite what I had learned in Montréal and Boston, Portland was the *real* start of my wrestling career. It was still the minor leagues, but because Don Owen was so good to his wrestlers, a lot of wrestlers wanted to work there. I was in Oregon for about eighteen months, wrestling in a real promotion, with television exposure and a regular circuit. And I was making a living.

Then one day in 1963 Don told me he was sending me to Texas. He explained I needed to get out so I would return fresh with new stories to tell. At that time, promoters were always trading guys, sending you somewhere else. I expected to be treated the same there as I had been in Portland, or at least like Boston. Once I got to Texas, I was starving. I was in for a rude awakening.

I bought a car for the first time to make the trip south. Louie and I left in it with everything we owned. The engine blew before my run in Texas ended. It was a real piece of crap, a big 1958 Lincoln. Years ago, cars would get very hot if you drove for long distances. And when you had to drive for miles and miles in the middle of the desert, on dirt roads since there were no highways, the car engine got very, very hot. Every 200 miles or so, you had a little place by the side of the road where you could buy food and water in a bag to keep the car cool. You would hook those to the back and front bumpers. If the car heated up in the middle of the desert, you could stop and put water in the radiator before anything bad happened. It's only been fifty years since then, but it seems like centuries ago.

On the day Louie and I were about 100 miles from the Texan border, we stopped in a shitty little place to eat because there wasn't anything else for miles around. We went to the bathroom and there were three little stalls. Two of them said white and one said black. It was a shock for us coming from Portland and even Boston, and yet we were still in the same country. My first night in Texas was in Beaumont. I finally found the arena and when I went to wrestle, I saw they had all the black fans in one area and all the white fans in another. It was a long time before they had a match with a white man against a black man. Eventually, promoters saw the money in that and things changed. I definitely wasn't in Portland anymore.

We worked in Houston, Dallas, Corpus Christi, and Austin, mostly in small arenas. Louie was alone a lot in Texas. The travel was too extensive, and I was barely home. The day we rented our apartment in Houston was the day John F. Kennedy visited: November 21, 1963. Louie even went to see him in person. The next day, the President was shot in Dallas.

The "Pretty Boy" gimmick didn't work in Texas and I pretty much dropped it after that. As far as the guys went, there was a clique in place and they wouldn't let me be part of the team. I kept developing my craft, but it was no fun wrestling with them, not like it had been in Boston or Portland.

My car blew up just as I was giving my two weeks' notice in Texas; I needed to get it fixed quickly if I wanted to leave. Some of the other guys from the territory told me about a mechanic who gave wrestlers a deal. A week later, my car was ready and I owed $350. I told the mechanic I would swing by later to pay him, but I never did. Back then you needed to survive — and moving on to the next territory was the only way to do that. I wasn't proud of it, but I had been so miserable in Texas, and I needed to get out. I was not expecting to go back there anytime soon, so I took my chances and got away with it.

After Texas, I spent three months in Arizona. I had to ask for a $200 advance just to put gas in my tank. The advance was to be paid back slowly, by taking off a little money from each payment. I was already behind, and I hadn't even competed in one match. It looked like I'd jumped from the frying pan into the fire by going to work there. And I had.

The only good thing was that I became the top guy. The first time I "main-evented Madison Square Garden" was . . . in Phoenix, Arizona. Shades of things to come, you might say. If the promoter, Ernie Mohammed, hadn't been a no-good bastard, things could have been good. I had a little leverage as the champion and I tried to use it by cussing him and forcing him to do the right thing. However, my own money situation got so bad that I held him up for a grand before dropping his championship to "Bulldog" Don Kent and leaving the territory. Imagine that, I was the champion and I was broke. It shows you how successful that piece of shit was as a promoter.

Louie and I stayed with one of the referees during that time. His name escapes me, but he was originally from Québec and he had a big house with orange and grapefruit trees in the yard. We would open our windows in the morning and pick fruit for breakfast. It doesn't get any fresher than that, does it? They had also had a stable and in the morning Louie and I would ride horses. We spent a lot of quality time like that over the years. Even though I wasn't making any money, we enjoyed at least part of our stay in Arizona. I like to think that's who I am — a person who finds some way to have fun no matter what. And, no matter what, it was an interesting life; I mean, it had to be a lot more fun than being yelled at in a factory, didn't it?

I went to Oklahoma next. Leroy McGuirk promoted the territory. Leroy was blind, and he had a matchmaker named Leo Voss. Leo also refereed house shows and took care of the money and all of that stuff. He was in charge of everything, like a producer on the road today with WWE. Everyone told me I should be careful around him. He had a reputation as a snitch who'd go back to Leroy with everything he saw on the road. But we actually became good friends and never had any issues. We hit it off right away and I just loved the guy.

McGuirk, on the other hand, gave me a rough time about screwing the Arizona promoter on my way out. He explained that if I did that again, promoters all around the country might stop booking me. But ultimately I did really well for him. The territory was built around "junior heavyweights," so at the time I was a perfect fit. Mike Clancy and Danny Hodge, the Olympic silver medalist, are two of the most well-known wrestlers from that territory that I was matched against for the next six months. I became a true star in that territory. I was the champion and I was getting real main-event money at last. It was no different then than it is today: if you're the champion and selling tickets, you make more money than the curtain jerker. It was quite the experience for Louie and me; it seemed like everyone wore a cowboy hat and, once again, we traveled small dirt roads through miles of desert just to get anywhere. The food was different, too. Your choices always seemed to be either barbecue or Mexican; for a kid from Montréal who had always eaten the same thing, it was eye-opening.

I was discovering the world with the man I loved, but I still didn't feel like I could bring him anywhere. Once again, Louie was stuck in our apartment, waiting for me to come home. Oklahoma was tough on him, even if it was a good place for me to work. In Texas, Arizona, and Oklahoma, I don't think anyone really knew that we were gay. Some guys might have suspected, but there were enough "smoke and mirrors" that no one was sure. When somebody asked me if I was a queer, I would always tell them to go to hell and play the tough guy.

There was a time, however, I was sure the truth would come out and I would be in trouble. Early one morning, one of the referees, an old-timer, knocked on our door. Louie opened it — in his underwear. The referee asked if I was there and he said yes. I pulled myself out of bed to speak with him. The message was simply that they needed me in the office at 2 p.m. that afternoon. No problem, I said. What I was soon to find out is that he immediately spread the rumor back at the office that my boyfriend had opened the door naked. It spread like wildfire; I found out before even going to the office that afternoon. When I got there, I was Mad Dog Vachon mad.

"Where is that goddamn asshole referee?" I yelled.

I proceeded to rant about the lie he spread about my friend Louie and me. I told everyone who'd listen that if the no-good son of a bitch showed his face, I would beat the hell out of him. I made sure Leo Voss, especially, knew I was serious.

"Please, Pat, don't do that. I will fix this," he said.

I yelled, still doing my best Mad Dog Vachon impression, "Why would he start shit like that? It's not true. He opened the door in his underwear. That's it. No story."

I was pissed off and made quite the scene. I wanted to show I was ready to fight if they tried to intimidate me.

Afterward, I started to regret how far I'd gone with my outburst. Maybe that referee was a friend of Danny Hodge. If he was, I wouldn't get to tour the territory competing against Hodge, who was a top guy, which meant I'd been out a lot of money that I desperately needed after Texas and Arizona. Worse, what if I did have to wrestle him? Was Hodge, who was legendarily tough, going to squeeze the living hell out of me? Remember, Louie and I were two men living together in Oklahoma in 1963. I didn't want to get blacklisted, or worse. I was a good professional wrestler, but I wasn't a tough guy. It turned out nothing happened, and I had a great time wrestling with Danny, who to this day is known for being able to squeeze apple juice out of an apple with his bare hands.

It was the same with Mike Clancy when he saw me compete — he wanted to work with me, too. It was beautiful wrestling with him, like fine craftsmanship. I had so much fun and learned so much; he even invited me to his house and everything. I had dinner with his family, but I could not bring Louie.

When I had had enough of the Oklahoma territory, I called Don Owen and asked if I could come back. He gave me a start date and, before I knew it, my career really took off. I was on top of the world as Pacific Northwest Champion.

I was fortunate to meet another great teacher when I returned to Portland. Maurice Vachon had moved out of the territory, and I was on my own. Pepper Martin was another Canadian, from Ontario. He later became an actor, and he's probably best known for his role in *Superman II* — he was the truck driver who sucker-punched Superman when the Man of Steel lost his power. Anyway, I was just coming back into the territory and we were watching each other wrestle. As he was coming back from the ring one night, I told him I couldn't wait to wrestle him. He said he felt the same way.

So obviously, the first match we had together we . . . completely sucked. He was trying to lead; I was trying to lead. After every move, we'd argue about what to do next. Finally, I asked him to just follow me and told him not to worry.

Whether I was the good guy or bad guy, I always worked best when I was the one leading the dance. Martin went to Don Owen and requested a series of matches with me. It was one hell of a program we worked together for the title. Yet what I remember most is something funny that occurred, and nothing to do with a championship bout.

In one particular match, I was supposed to hit Martin with some brass knuckles. I was trying to hide them from view, and the referee grabbed me so hard that they went flying into the crowd. Martin and I both dove outside the ring to get the object as though we were competing for a gold medal. We were able to get them back just in time before a fan had a good look. We were scared out of our minds. I can laugh about it now, but back then protecting the business was often the most important part of our job.

Another memorable match was one I had with an interesting stipulation: if you lost, you had to ride a donkey out of the building. It was just like the wild west, back when they would literally run people out of town. It was epic — I wonder why we've never done it in WWE.

There were many wannabe promoters in those days, most of them moonlighting in the role, running a small town. I'm told there are still people doing the same thing today. One of them booked me in a haircut match: I lost and had to shave my head bald. In theory, the gimmick was supposed to generate extra cash for everyone. The promoter presented it this way: "If you do it, maybe we'll get a better house next time?" That meant a bigger cut for me. Ultimately, I think I wound up making fifty dollars a night instead of forty.

I started to wear a mask to hide my baldness from the fans. I didn't get a bonus for it, mind you, but people went crazy whenever an opponent would try to unmask me to expose my bald head. One night in a small town just outside of Portland, we worked a mask match like this and I lost, but the people didn't see me without the mask. No payoff kept the crowd hot. But the promoter had taken a picture of me backstage and, without my knowledge, sent the picture to the newspapers. When I found that out, I did my best Mad Dog impression again: "Why would you do that?"

"People were really mad because they didn't get to see you bald."

"Sure, they were mad, you dumb shit. That's why they were going to come back next week."

Because of him, we never had that return bout and we lost that payoff. It still pisses me off today.

One guy I learned a lot from was Nick Kozak. He was a great worker and I wrestled with him more times than I can count. He would have me put him into a hold and insist I keep him down, not let go. He wanted me to really dominate so that he could sell it and get the crowd behind him. Then he would get me to let him stand up, only to follow up by pulling his hair and putting him down again. The fans would go damn near crazy. This guy could sell like you would not believe. When he made a comeback, the crowd jumped to their feet. My God, he was great. And this is how I really learned how this business worked. He wasn't selfish; he knew that if he wanted his comeback to mean something, he needed to give me a lot of offense. Normally, guys don't want to wait that long before they get their turn to shine. He was a great teacher.

Years later, when we were in Houston for *Monday Night Raw* just before *WrestleMania X-7*, I received a call. I don't know how Nick Kozak got my number, but I'm glad he did. I got him front-row seats for *Raw*. I brought him backstage and introduced him to Vince. He was happy to meet Nick, because I had told him many times how the guy had really helped me learn the business when I was a kid. Vince told him, "I want to thank you from the bottom of my heart for what you did for the business. If you want to come back for *WrestleMania*

X-7 bring anyone you want; you'll be my guest." It made me feel real good to give a little something back to Nick Kozak all those years later. He's in his eighties now and he still looks great.

Being back in Portland was also good for Louie. He was accepted there, a part of everything because of the time we'd spend hanging out with Mad Dog. There was one gay bar where we could be together without hiding. It was great to enjoy ourselves outside of the business and we even made some gay friends. It was the polar opposite of the previous year when I was on the road working Southern territories. In Oregon, Louie had friends and he could go to the bar with them when I was on the road for a long time. He was also working and meeting new people on his own. Louie was one hell of a dancer. He knew all the ballroom dances, waltzes and that sort of thing. Louie found a job teaching dance to women and he loved that job like crazy. He was making extra money and that made him happy, too.

When he got tired of teaching, he got a job as a busboy at a very nice downtown hotel. Well, *tabarnak*, after a week there they made him a waiter because he was great with all the upscale parties. I was wrestling for thirty-five dollars a night at the time and as it turned out he was making fifty a night on tips alone. He was making more money than I was. He did that for a long time.

On the wrestling front, I embarked on a two-year run for Don Owen. In the process, I started to carve out a name for myself that really meant something in the business. Owen would bring in Lou Thesz, the World Champion, once a year. When I got to work with him, I was in heaven. He's one of the greatest of all time, and I learned a lot from those experiences as well.

It was never quite like in Boston, but I always enjoyed Portland and the wrestlers would inevitably have a good laugh. I remember the guy who would bring our jackets back to the dressing room.

Every time he did, someone would yell "Kayfabe." It was common practice each time an outsider entered the sanctuary that was our dressing room to yell that code word. It simply meant we should not be talking about business. That went on a few times each night for several weeks. Then one night, the guy decided to stand up for himself and told the whole dressing room: "I don't mind the yelling, but I want to let you know that my name is not Kayfabe. It's Mark."

We all burst out laughing and told him we'd call him Mark from then on with tears in our eyes. What he didn't know is that wrestlers called people outside of the business "marks" — that's why we were yelling kayfabe in the first place.

Another interesting person I met during that time was a Japanese wrestler called Kazimoto. It was my job to take care of him while he was in town, so he traveled with me everywhere. I knew of a Japanese restaurant in Portland — now they're everywhere, but back then they were hard to find. I took him there so he could feel a bit more at home and he went on to eat at the place every goddamn day, every meal. He was with us for about six months. I took good care of him and said a pleasant goodbye to him when he left. I had no idea I was going to work in Japan someday; I just wanted to be nice and help him. Many years later, I ended up wrestling in Japan. While I was waiting for the train with some other wrestlers, bad guys on one side and all the good guys on the other side, I spotted this tall man with the group on the other side. I asked the other wrestlers the big guy's name.

"It's Inoki," someone said. "He's the big star here. Don't mess with him."

I knew better: that's not Inoki. I wrestled that guy in Portland: his name is Kazimoto.

That night I sneaked into the babyfaces' dressing room. We really were not allowed to do that in Japan; they insisted on separate dressing rooms. I snatched him aside and asked, "You remember me?"

"It's you, Patterson, with blond hair," he said.

From that point on, I was taken care of like you would not believe. I never had a problem in the ring or out while working in Japan. We respected each other as human beings and as wrestlers, despite our cultural differences. While working for Vince Sr. later on, I flew to Tokyo from New York to wrestle Inoki in a sixty-minute television match, then flew right back to New York the same night. No hotel, no restaurant, just airports and the arena. Coincidently, Inoki was inducted into the WWE Hall of Fame at the same time as Mad Dog.

In Oregon, it may rain every two days, but they also have mountains nearby. Louie and I went skiing a few times and loved it. We made a lot of friends and our life was good. But after a long run, it was time for me to move on. Portland was a small territory and I had done everything that could be done. Roy Shire promoted in San Francisco, California, and Pepper Martin kept telling me I should go there — that I was a perfect fit. Louie and I felt that the more clement weather was worth risking our cozy life in Oregon. Pepper told me, "You have the style that Roy Shire likes." And that helped convince me. I had heard a lot about his star, Ray Stevens, and a few of the guys actually said that if we tagged, we would be the greatest team of all time. Talk about putting on the pressure, but Shire had a good reputation and it was a big territory.

I finally called him.

"Hello, it's Pat Patterson."

"Yeah, what can I do for you?" he said in his best grumpy old man voice.

"I would love to come to work for you. I have been in Oregon for two years now, and I am on top and doing good business. Some of the guys told me I would be a great partner for Ray Stevens."

He shouted, "The wrestlers don't decide what I do. *I decide.*"

Right away I backtracked, saying I was not telling him what to do, just offering my services. He used to team with Ray Stevens himself, when Ray played his "brother" Ray Shire. He might have been sensitive about anyone else being partnered with Ray. He snapped that I should send pictures and hung up.

It was not what I expected at all. Still I knew if I wanted to make it, I needed to go to a bigger territory. If I made it there, I would be a real top guy. So I took the chance, just like I had when I moved to Boston. I knew things were about to get interesting, I just had no idea how interesting.

READY FOR MY CLOSE-UP

"Regrets, I've had a few, but then again, too few to mention"

Want to know something funny? When I decided we were going to move to San Francisco and Big Time Wrestling in 1965, I had no idea the city had a large and vibrant gay community. Louie and I were quick learners, however, and we enjoyed life in California for a long time. San Francisco is a fantastic city, one of my favorites in the whole world, and being gay was never an issue there . . . Now if I could just change the promoter's mind . . .

My first match in the new territory was for a television taping in Fresno. Roy Shire, the promoter, was a former wrestler and he told me he'd pick me up and take me there himself. The very first thing he said to me was "I heard you're different."

"How so, Mr. Shire?"

"I heard you're a queer."

That's it for me, I thought, I'm not going to be here long. "I will be honest with you, sir, I will work hard and I will never embarrass you. As for the rest, I prefer gay."

"OK. But you look like shit. You should start working out."

When I got home, I told Louie that Shire didn't like gay people and that I wasn't sure what the future held for us in the Bay area. And then I decided to start going to the gym — because I was definitely not going to embarrass him.

It's funny how things work out. Louie and I ended up getting our first home in San Francisco. And I wound up making truly good money for the first time. We stayed there on and off for almost fourteen years. And I helped a homophobic promoter turn a healthy profit.

Despite his early prejudice, I learned the business side of wrestling from Roy Shire. He was one of the few true geniuses of the sport. Even if we had our differences at the end, I appreciated the opportunity to learn the psychology of wrestling from him.

My first match at the Cow Palace, the biggest arena in the territory, was against Red Bastien. He was a fantastic performer, who wrestled elsewhere full-time but lived in San Francisco. Every once in a while, he would come in to be with his family. We tore the house down; people were going banana when I won the match. When we got back to the dressing room, Bastien looked at Shire and said, "Holy shit, where the hell did you get this guy?"

That he said it in front of everybody in the dressing room was important. You can't overestimate what it meant to have a respected veteran like Bastien say something like that. It wasn't long before I was tag-teaming with Ray Stevens as part of the Blond Bombers. I got my hair dyed blond for the first time in San Francisco to fit better with Ray. We had an almost instant chemistry and we were recognized as one of the best tag teams in the business for a long time. Backstage the other wrestlers also loved us, because we were there to have fun. There was no politics and no bullshit with us. Ultimately, Ray was just like me, except he was crazy about women.

(I have a full chapter of Ray Stevens stories in Chapter Eight. Skip ahead if you wish. I will still be here when you return.)

(Hope you enjoyed my Ray Stevens stories; I just loved the man.)

Many Quebecers have had good wrestling careers in America, but most were also limited because of their inability to do a good interview in English. One Friday night when I first arrived in Portland, Don Owen told me to go to the balcony: I had five minutes to talk.

I think I said, "Me don't speak English?"

He told me it didn't matter, that I should just say whatever I could. I was terrible. I would say I was the best and I would fake jumping over the balcony. I would do anything to try to get a reaction. I would yell, half in French and half in English, until I finally got it. I hated cutting promos at first, because I sounded like an idiot most of the time. Each time I got a little better and by the time I made it to San Francisco, I'd started to get it. But I needed to be thrown out there to learn. Not a lot of what I did in San Francisco survives on video, but a fan used to record the audio from television, so I have a few of those recordings to help me remember the good old days.

The first time I ever watched wrestling on television in Montréal, the voice of the show was Michel Normandin. The program was promoted by Eddie Quinn. I saw a retiring Yvon Robert teach his heir apparent Johnny Rougeau the Japanese hammerlock. It's funny which memories stick with you. There were a few more Quebecers on the tube: Ovila Asselin, Larry Moquin, Bob Langevin, and Omer Marchessault. Never in a million years did I imagine being on TV like them. It was always fun to have people from Québec come into the territory. I guess Maurice Vachon rubbed off on me the right way.

One of my favorite visitors from *la belle province* was midget star Sky Low Low. Crazy things happened when he was drunk, and we'd often play pranks on him when he went to the restroom. Stupid shit mostly: I would sit on his hat "by mistake" and then he would make a big scene. As always, it was all about having a big laugh. One time on the road, I went to his room late at night. When he opened the door, I pulled him out into the hall and locked him out of his room, buck-naked. As I fled the scene of the crime, I had to stop in the stairs because I was laughing so hard. When I got to the lobby, the clerk wanted to know what was going on. I told him to just wait — while I hid in the corner. Who exited the elevator? A naked Sky Low Low, acting like nothing was out of the ordinary.

Another time, Sky was drinking in the bar across the street and had passed out. Two cops came in who knew all the wrestlers. I asked them to play a prank on him. "Just tell him you are sending him to jail as you wake him up. Don't worry, he will get angry, but that will be it, and it will be funny." The joke turned bad, however, and Sky went berserk. I found it funnier that way, but the cops didn't feel the same way.

Another time we were playing pool when I took some water from a fountain in the room. The next time I passed by Sky I faked a sneeze and threw that water on him. He chased me all around the bar with his pool cue.

This was our everyday life on the road: playing jokes and having fun. When I would ride in the car with Sky, I would always get him mad. He would yell and scream all the time. Man, what I put that poor guy through. There were no limits to what we would do to each other for a laugh on the road. I used to buy small padlocks and hook them behind a new guy's license plate, so they would hear them clicking for hours before figuring out what was going on. It would drive them nut. I never pulled a joke to be mean, or to get someone in trouble. It was always done for everyone to have a good laugh.

When you drive all the time like that, or fly from city to city, you don't really think about it. You just want to get to the next town. When you start looking back, all that travel doesn't make much sense. I think that's why I loved California, we were home almost every night. We could have a life and enjoy it. Some of the wrestlers liked getting booked in places like Hawaii for two or three months to get a vacation from the road. They didn't make a lot of money but they were on the beach every day with their wives. That wasn't for me. I did go there with Ray Stevens as part of the Blond Bombers, but we never stayed for more than two weeks at a time. Ray always made those trips memorable, one way or another.

The Cow Palace was a dangerous arena, and it was a long walk to the damn ring. The aisles were very narrow, with fans always almost touching us. Security guards wore riot gear and often swatted at fans with billy clubs. Back in the day, there were no barricades, and when you came down the aisle, people — even the women — would kick at you and spit on you. One night in San Francisco, a lady took her hatpin and stabbed me with it. It stayed stuck in my shoulder until I reached the dressing room. I was in pain and I was mad. It wasn't a big injury, but I was so pissed. We had little patience with fans who would do something like that. We were always in danger; fans scratched my car on a regular basis and I had to get good at finding hidden or secret parking spots. Sometimes, driving on the highway, they would even throw beer bottles. They were trying to kill me.

In San Francisco, some fans discovered where I lived and threw rocks at my windows. It was serious in my day: bad guys today don't know what real heat is. Heat is a business term, and it means how much people hate you. In my day, there was actually such a thing as too much heat.

In San Jose one night, I wasn't taking any chances and I got to the show real early and parked my car three blocks away from the arena. No one saw me come in. But after the show, I still needed help to get out. I had heat like you would not believe — it was actually dangerous. People were waiting for us villains, and to get at me in particular.

That night I strategized my escape with one of the referees: "Here is my key; go out the front door and walk three blocks west and you will see my car. Then come by the building and pick me up. I will be in the lobby and I will look for you and jump in as soon as you are there. Then get us out fast."

As soon as he showed up, I ran for the car like I was at the Olympics. But when I got there, the door was locked. I was pleading for him to open the damn door, but he couldn't find the button. By the time he did, it was too late. I was already running down the street and the fans were already throwing rocks at me. I took refuge in a nearby hotel lobby of the Sainte Claire. They literally were throwing *shit* at me that day. Someone from the hotel had to call the police so I could leave. When *WrestleMania 31* was on the West Coast in 2015, I went back to visit the same hotel, now the Westin San Jose, because it was near where we were staying and such an architectural treasure for the city.

Another time I was driving to a show in Eureka, California, in my brand-new Cadillac. I employed the same strategy and parked three blocks away. Only this time, I gave the ref the night off and had the police escort me back to my car after the show. When I got there, I had two flat tires and my Cadillac was all scratched up. I got pissed when things like that happened. The promoter would get us security sometimes, but would never pay the bill.

I would tell Roy that some of the stuff we did was creating too much heat for me. He would say, "Patterson, if you can't take the heat, get out of the kitchen." That was a big help. Thanks, Roy.

It's unbelievable the lengths people would go to back in the late sixties. And when you think about it, everything we used to do for wrestling was stupid. We would defend the business to the point of getting in trouble with the law or, worse, putting our lives at risk. We're lucky there was never a real tragedy — even though some wrestlers were stabbed with knives instead of hatpins. Actually, I was lucky it never escalated. We all had short tempers, though I kept mine in check most of the time.

One night in Sacramento, however, it wasn't a fan I had trouble with. We were working with an athletic commission referee. Those guys never liked it when we tried to create heat with them. On this occasion, I was using the official, a former wrestler and boxer, to make the match more intense. It got out of hand. When the match was over, he was really furious. I was more than a little worried: he could be a tough son of a bitch and I was definitely not. I decided to stand my ground against him in the dressing room and prepared to fight. Because the truth was if he hit me first, I was done. Just as I thought, he came at me. I welcomed him with a chair shot to the head and split him wide open. At that point, the other wrestlers came in to pull us apart. When we cooled down, we both apologized. That's the kind of stuff that sometimes happened. It was my only dressing room fight, and I'm glad it was. I'm not a fighter, but we all had to be able to defend ourselves in certain situations.

I was lucky and I was careful; I didn't do stupid things like that too often. Still, San Francisco was the one place where I became so hated that it became dangerous for me outside of wrestling. When I finally became a good guy — a babyface — it all went away. (I will get to that later; don't worry.)

In 1969, while I was still working in San Francisco, I was sent to Amarillo for a few months. I had a good time there, too. Roy was good friends with the Funk family, who owned the territory. He wanted me to go there for four months to learn something new. I had a blast in Texas: the Funk brothers, Terry and Dory, are great guys. (The whole family is crazy, just like me.)

Though I was in Texas again, it definitely was not the same territory I'd worked during my first visit. This Texas experience felt more like a vacation. The drawback was still the long ride between towns, almost 300 miles between each venue. Louie traveled with me on these road trips, but it wasn't much better for him than during our first stay in Texas. Still, while we were in Amarillo, Louie went to barber school. Later on, when we were back in San Francisco, Louie had no problem taking the course to get his California barber's license.

It was also in Amarillo where, one night, I was the last one out of the building and I found a dog. It was a dark and cold evening, as a night in Texas can be at the wrong time of year. So there I was face-to-face with this nice little puppy, and it was shaking, and there was nobody for miles around. I felt bad for the poor thing and I put it in my car to bring it home. Right away, Louie said, "You're not keeping the dog."

"No, no, you're right. I'll get rid of it. Don't worry."

Louie had to leave early for barber school the next day. I was still sleeping and I could hear the dog crying. I rolled over onto my other side and it was all wet. The little bastard had shit my bed, and I was rolling in it. This was the end for this particular puppy and me. I gave it to somebody the same day. Much later, Louie and I finally had dogs in San Francisco. But at that time there was enough shit in the wrestling business — I didn't need to willingly roll into more in my own bed.

Life on the road was such that you'd look for little distractions just to keep yourself entertained. In Odessa, Texas, in the middle of nowhere, the wrestlers always stayed at the same hotel. We spent the day by the pool, wrestled at night, and then we'd move on to the next town the following day. Why that particular place? There was a local couple who used to invite wrestlers to participate in some special "after dark activities." The husband liked to watch while she did her thing with the wrestlers. They invited me to be a part of the action on a regular basis, but I would politely turn them down. Still, they liked me. They would bring food and beer, so we socialized quite a bit. There is nothing like offering something free if you want to interact with a wrestler. At the time, there was this wrestler from Mexico with us; he was a real nice guy and he had the hots for the woman. One day, he asked me to go with him so that he might have a chance to be intimate with her. Always there for my fellow wrestler, I told him that I would go, but that I would only watch with the husband.

When the time came, my friend was really putting in the effort; her head was off the bed and there was a good risk they might actually fall off. I decided to get up and "help" a little, making sure she would not fall off. So I am face-to-face with him and we are both doing our thing with her, and I see he is about to finish as he is moaning and screaming. I brushed his hair back and said, "Give me a kiss."

He stopped everything right there. He was so mad; he wanted to kill me for ruining the mood. Me, I was laughing. If I was going to help, I deserved at least a good laugh for my effort. I was not sexually attracted to women, but life is so short you might as well try everything when you have the chance. (There's more on that in Chapter Eight, and if you have not read that Ray Stevens chapter yet, you once again have my permission to go do so. The rest of this chapter will still be here when you're done.)

(Back already? Good, let's continue.)

In Amarillo, I wrestled against the promoter Dory Funk Sr. It was such an important match: heavyweight boxing champion Joe Louis was booked as the special guest referee. Let me tell you, I would never want to take a punch from that man, because if I had, my head would have fallen off my shoulders. He had the biggest wrists and hands I had ever seen. I learned a lot during my time in Texas, but after four months, I was ready to go back to California.

San Francisco is still one of my top places in the world, and if I have a favorite *anything*, there is a good chance you will find it in that city. I learned so much and truly enjoyed my life with Louie in the Bay area. I discovered many great restaurants and so much more of the finer things in life there. I was enjoying life to the fullest, and I was also becoming a star and reaching unbelievable success in my chosen profession.

Louie had opened up a barbershop. One day, there was a party at Roy Shire's house and he told me to ask Louie to bring his scissors so he could get a haircut. I told Roy to talk with Louie directly. So Roy called and asked him, but Louie didn't want to work at a party, so he told him to come by the barbershop instead. Roy was mad, saying that my damn friend Louie was a no-good son of a bitch. And do you know what the old man did? It took a month, but he finally wound up going to the barbershop. Louie told him his hair looked awful and he gave him a great haircut. Roy went back every month after that. He even gave him a good tip — and let me tell you, Roy was very tight with his money. Even Louie would tease him, saying that it must have really hurt Roy to give such a good tip. Louie was like that: he would never bullshit you; you'd get an honest opinion every time. That's why everyone loved him.

One thing you need to know about the way Roy Shire ran Big Time Wrestling: Louie had to buy a ticket if he wanted to see the show at the Cow Palace. Even Ray Stevens's wife had to buy a ticket. Shire would always say, "Does the mailman bring his wife to work? I'm running a business." By making Roy come to his barbershop, Louie was just following the same business principle.

A funny story: Roy used to try to impress everyone he met by making everything he did or was involved in sound so much better than it really was. Louie went off on him the very first time they met. "Who the hell are you?" he said. It was an explosive beginning, but they had a great relationship after that. Even if neither one of them ever gave away anything for free.

Another time Roy was hosting a party, he wanted Louie to act as the bartender.

"Why don't you ask Louie yourself?" I said.

When Roy finally reached out to him, Louie bluntly asked, "Are you inviting me to be at your party or do you want me there to just work as the bartender?"

"I need a bartender," Roy said.

"Well, Roy, you're gonna have to pay me then," said Louie.

Roy was shocked whenever Louie talked to him like that. Promoters weren't used to being told no. But at the end of the day, Roy paid him. While the party was going on, he asked Louie not to put so much alcohol in the drinks. Louie said, "I am the bartender. You need to be someplace else."

It's the truth, I swear; Louie was amazing. Why do you think I spent forty years of my life with him?

Moving to San Francisco made a huge difference to our lifestyle. I went from wrestling in front of 2,000 or 3,000 fans to performing in front of three, four, and often even five times as many people at the Cow Palace. We had a beautiful Spanish house. I paid $38,000 for it; it's probably worth over half a million dollars today, if not more. We made good money for the time, but still it was nothing like what the top guys make now. Guys today have it much better than we did. In WWE, there's guaranteed money, and you get paid even if you're hurt. The company will take care of your medical bills. Now some guys still spend their money too recklessly — that hasn't changed from my day. I learned quickly to take care of mine.

Our mountainside house in San Francisco was beautiful. I had a big pool and I had never experienced anything like it. We would throw parties and invite people to stay the night. Then I realized that if I made a sandwich for myself, I needed to make one for everyone. And I would buy vodka and beer and share that with everyone. It soon became expensive. We continued to throw parties but after a while we asked everyone to bring their own food and beverages. My friend's father had a big butcher shop, and he would bring these wonderful juicy steaks and pork chops. It was insane the food we would cook. Sometimes the party would be in full swing when I left to work and would still be going when I returned.

I began golfing in San Francisco. Louie was one hell of a player and he introduced me to the game. At first, I wasn't very good at it but I kept at it and started to love playing, I found it relaxing and a good way to escape life on the road. I still play on a regular basis. Back in the day, Bobby Heenan never wanted to play with us. He finally came out and used my old clubs. They were in bad shape; the grips were loose and Bobby kept complaining about them. Then out of nowhere, he sank a hole in one. He said that's it, I can't get any better, and stopped playing for the rest of the day. Bobby is the best.

Louie and I brought both of our families out to spend time with us in San Francisco and share in our success. We had so much fun with them. Louie's dad would cook. My dad had never met a chef like him before. He made big bowls of pasta with homemade sauce and everything. This is probably one of my proudest and fondest memories, to be able to share those moments with both our families like that. One day, Louie and I sent our dads out to use the tramway. We told them to go down the line and enjoy the city. Well, next thing I know, Louie's father was telling me that my dad's a dirty old man. Apparently, they'd used their time in the city to watch a porno movie. We had a good laugh about that — they were having such a good time, as if they were both teenagers. We dressed our dads up in my wrestling gear, with the championship and everything, and took pictures. And though we were spending a lot of quality time together, my dad and I never really managed to get any closer. Even though we were having fun, and even traveled to some towns together, we could not fix the past. When I would visit Montréal after that, however, Dad wanted me to visit all our relatives and bring pictures to show them I was a champion. It was just a case of "too little, too late." My mother seemed like she was in tears all the time — she was proud of my success, but even prouder of me.

I took my parents to see me wrestle in San Francisco, Reno, and Las Vegas. We flew from San Francisco to Vegas. It was a forty-five-minute journey on Western Airlines which, at the time, was known as the "Champagne Airline." As soon as the plane took off, everyone over twenty-one was given a glass of champagne. My mom and dad never drank. My mom said, "What's that?"

"It's champagne."

"Champagne?"

"Yeah, champagne; it's free."

"No, champagne is not free."

"Ma, it's free."

"You're spending too much money."

"Ma, it's free. I'm not spending any money."

She didn't believe me. Anyway, they finally began sipping their drinks and, before you know it, she was talking loudly and crying a little. Soon she was turning red and I knew she had a buzz on. I said, "Ma, please don't worry about anything."

She just couldn't accept it. When the stewardess walked by, she asked me, "Is the lady OK?"

"Yes," I said, "she's fine. She doesn't believe it's free champagne because she thinks it's too expensive."

"Oh, she'll be all right, don't worry." And then the stewardess went to the back of the plane. When she returned, she put a whole bottle of champagne on the table.

"Now you're overdoing it!" my mom said. But she kept that bottle of champagne.

I took my parents to a famous drag queen show, a big tourist attraction in San Francisco. I knew everybody there, so we were sitting in the first row, center stage. My father could not wrap his mind around the fact that they were men dressed as women.

"I am telling you, Dad, they're men."

They had never seen anything close to that in Montréal. Before we went, Louie treated my mother to a complete makeover — and I mean complete, including dyeing her hair and applying fake eyelashes. My mom was funny and said, "Everyone is going to think that I am the one disguised as a woman."

My mother had never been treated to anything like that, and she was gorgeous. She deserved it and I'm glad I was able to provide her with a little magic on nights like that. My parents had no idea I was doing so well until they saw it for themselves. I had to explain that performing at the Cow Palace was like wrestling in the main event at the Forum, that I was just like Yvon Robert. They were amazed: Robert was a big star in my hometown, a symbol for all French Canadians because of his popularity and success.

When they first came to our house, we had a king-size bed for them to sleep in. They had never seen a king-size bed in their life, let alone slept in one. The first morning, they slept in. I heard my mother asking my dad what time it was; he told her to keep sleeping, that it didn't matter. I was not going to let that opportunity pass me by. I changed each and every clock in the house by two hours. They woke up around 10 a.m., but when my dad checked the time, the clock indicated it was noon.

"*Ben voyons, Gérard, ça pas de bon sens dormir tard de même!*" My God, Gérard, we can't do that — sleep in that late!

I was laughing my ass off. They hurried downstairs to the living room, trying to figure out how it could have happened. We explained the joke, but Louie and I had a good laugh about that for a long time. They stayed for three weeks, and I brought them everywhere with me. Later on, Louie's parents moved closer to us, just outside of San Francisco. We saw each other quite often until his dad died. Soon after, and just before Louie and I left for Florida, his mom passed away, too.

We often vacationed in Boston and stayed with Louie's sister. When we were in town, we made sure to see the nephews and the nieces play hockey and baseball — all the things a family would do. We were simply called Uncle Pat and Uncle Louie. I love them a lot, and they've brought me great joy over the years. I am very proud of them.

If things had been different, I would have loved to have children with Louie. I love children very much, and Louie did as well. Louie had such a good heart, and he'd talk for hours and hours with a child. I don't know, if we'd had the option back then, maybe we would have considered adopting. A little girl, maybe. But it was a different time and my career always came first, and it would probably not have been a good idea. Louie knew that, too, and he accepted it. I always said, "What comes first is not you or us. It's the business. And it's always going to be that way. If I am successful in the business, we are going to live well. Business comes first. When I need to go on the road, or spend months in Japan, don't bitch. I will always come back to you." I was lucky — he accepted that and at home we never talked about wrestling. We were perfect for each other.

Still, we had so much love we could have given to a child. I always liked the Big Brothers and Big Sisters organizations. You can treat a child to an amazing day by taking him or her to the circus or simply out to eat some ice cream. But I never even applied. I would have had to say I was gay, and back then people associated gay men with pedophiles. So I didn't see the point in subjecting myself to that. Still, I am sure the kids would have had a great time. This might be one of the few regrets of my life, not to have been able to give a child all the good things I never had as a kid. Louie and I could have done so many good things for kids who needed it, if we had been allowed. But that's life. I don't like having regrets — and even if I have a few, I don't dwell on the past.

Pat Patterson is certainly not a unique name in America. In Oakland, there was a car dealer with the same name. I've been asked if I am him quite often, but strangely I have never met him or any other Pat Patterson in all of my travels. I've heard stories about quite a few people calling his dealerships to ask if he was a wrestler. And hey, even if there's more than one Pat Patterson out there, I'm still unique.

When I turned and became a good guy, I was finally able to start giving a little back to my community. One time, I was invited to visit sick children in a San Francisco hospital. As wrestlers, we were famous, but many of the kids still had no idea who we were. The show we did was not really geared toward children. When they brought me to visit a section of the hospital where older people were staying, things were different. Now those people *had* seen me on television. I took pictures with everyone and then approached a blind woman sitting in the corner all by herself. She said, "I can't believe I'm talking to Pat Patterson. I can't believe I'm touching your hand. When they put the TV on, I can hear you talk."

I don't know why but she really touched me. Maybe I saw a little of my mother in her. I asked the nurse and the other medical personnel how long she had been at the hospital. They told me she had

I don't have a lot of regrets, but I sometimes wonder, what if Louie and I had had a child together?

been there for years and that she had no family. I asked if I could take her out one day, and they said sure. I brought her to the beach in my convertible. She felt the fresh air and heard the sounds of the waves; the warmth of the sun on her skin made her realize where she was. We had an amazing day.

I had fought the idea of becoming a good guy for a long time. The old-timers would always say to me that I was a good-looking kid and that I should be a good guy, but I resisted. And I guess that's why I became an ass-kicking good guy: I like being the villain too much. I was in San Francisco for so long, it was bound to happen at some point. And I took advantage of it when it did.

There were some benefits to being a fan favorite. I was free to hang around other wrestlers who were also popular. I became good friends with Rocky Johnson and Peter Maivia. Before when I would fight Maivia at the Cow Palace, all the Samoans wanted to kill me because of the beating I would give him. I was calling his wife, Leah, and asking if she could get the Samoans seats anywhere but ringside for those shows. Seriously, I was legitimately scared for my life. I was sure they were going to kill me some day. Even when she managed to get them seated at the top of the arena, as soon as Peter got into trouble they would come down ringside. No one could stop them — they're truly a force of nature. Remember, I'm not a tough guy; I just played one on TV. If they only knew how frightened I was.

I wrestled Rocky Johnson a lot and we had great matches together. He was really popular and a very fine performer. The only thing was that he could be a little lazy sometimes . . . So one time I grabbed him by the hair and told him to stop being a lazy bastard. I ended up pulling out some of his hair.

"Get mad, you son of a bitch," I said, knowing I had to get him hot for him to give me his best. But when I did, man, was it good.

When we see each other now, he always says we tore it down.

And my response to that is always the same: "Yeah, because I chewed your ass."

While I was teaming with Peter Maivia, I was finally invited to party at his place. Because before, obviously, I had been a hated rival. At the first party I attended, I looked around and there were at least fifty Samoans who all looked like Afa and Sika staring at me intensely. In fact, most of them were the same people who used to scare me to death when Peter and I were mortal enemies — back when I actually used to leave the Cow Palace *hidden in a box* to escape them. Concerned, I asked Leah if I was OK. She told me not to worry, that they were not going to touch me.

"Are you sure? Because they look like they want to kill me and burn my body."

But it turned out she was right. I was fine. Thank God.

Back when I was in Oregon, main-event matches were two out of three falls. In between falls, you had to go back to the dressing room. Imagine what that was like for us villains: we had just beat up the fan's favorite and people are screaming for revenge and we could barely walk to the back because there were no barricades to keep people away from us. After a short break of five or six minutes, we had to do it all over again to get back into the ring so that the match could proceed. Often I barely reached the dressing room before it was time to go back. I'm telling you, guys have it easy today. And San Francisco was even worse than Portland. People would jump us in the ring — there must have been nearly fifty people trying to get to us one night. I was scared many times, but that specific night I was sure I was going to die. If you want to read more about that night, well, you're going to have to finish this chapter first. I'll tell you all about it in Chapter Eight . . .

Even if it was occasionally scary, it was still a wonderful time in my life. As a top wrestler, life is great — you just need to be careful.

Rocky Johnson was dating Ata, Peter and Leah's daughter. Eventually she became pregnant, and it seemed like all the Samoans wanted to kill him. I had to play peacemaker and get everyone to accept the situation. When that baby was born, they called him Dwayne. (I always felt they should have called him Pat, but that's just me.)

I would fight Dwayne's dad and grandfather, and then his mom would bring him backstage and I would bounce the baby Rock on my knees. It was an experience in the powerful cycle of life . . . Just as it was later when I would work with that same baby boy, now a man, as he headlined *WrestleMania*.

Looking back, I was blessed to gain the trust of my colleagues everywhere I went, and lucky to be matched against some of the best wrestlers from the get-go. I learned so much from them. When I became more seasoned myself, other guys would come to *me* to help them with their matches. I think it was because they didn't want to have to talk to Roy Shire, who was yelling most of the time.

I never minded people criticizing or teaching me — as long as they weren't yelling at me.

There is no goddamn reason to yell. If you explain what I did wrong, I can learn. I will never forget this: when I first started wrestling main events in San Francisco, no one ever told me there was anything wrong with my shit. And then finally, after watching my match, a dear friend of mine, Pedro Morales, and I had this conversation.

"*Amigo*, we need to talk. You are the best goddamn villain I have ever seen wrestle, but that goddamn thing you do in the corner . . . Your kicks? Your kicks look like shit."

"What?"

"Your kicks in the corner look like shit."

Thank you, Pedro.

Nobody ever wants to tell the top guy what he's doing wrong. I've never forgotten that moment. He was my friend, and because he was my friend, he was ready to tell me the truth. Now, don't get me wrong: that doesn't mean I wouldn't try to play a joke on my friend . . .

During a battle royal, everyone is in the ring. Well, one night, Pedro was booked in one and I wasn't. Alone in the locker room, I took a big padlock and put it on Pedro's bag. Probably not my smartest move, because, let me tell you, you don't mess with Pedro Morales. No one else would dare play a joke on him. Each time someone was eliminated from that match, they came through the curtain and saw me: I gave them feedback on what they'd done in the ring, as usual, so no one would suspect me. When Pedro came to the back and saw his bag, he went crazy. He threw his bag and chairs everywhere.

"Nobody touches my shit," he said, furious.

Everyone was looking at Mr. Fuji at that point, because he was usually the guilty party in that type of situation. Fuji looked at me, asking with his eyes if it was me. I made sure he understood it wasn't by asking him the same question the same way. I never found out what Pedro did with his bag that day, but we did laugh about it. Today the truth can finally be told.

Roy Shire, however, was never a laughing matter. Roy was different. No matter how good you were in the ring, he didn't care about your moves. All that mattered to him was the psychology. He didn't care if you did something spectacular, he cared if it *meant* something.

I'm grateful that I learned that from him, because that's my role today. I get to talk with the top guys and tell them what they did wrong or what they can improve upon, the stuff no one else will have the balls to tell them. And I love my job. Because a lot of the guys want to learn and they want to know how to get better and do things right.

With Shire in San Francisco, I started to work for the office, helping to run shows in some towns for the first time. Strangely enough, I never had a problem with the wrestlers not wanting to do what I needed them to do. I realized that this was something I enjoyed very much, because of the creativity involved, almost right away. I was lucky that I'd learned and understood the right way to do this kind of thing because of experience. Some people spend their life in the business and will never get it, because they only see things from a personal perspective, because it's always about them. With the broader view of my understanding of what's best for business, I could transition to working backstage once my in-ring career was over.

Wrestlers need feedback, and if you want to be a good teacher, you need to build trust with them by telling them both what's right about their performance and, more importantly, what's wrong. Today, I'm no longer in charge of specific talent or matches, but, often enough, one of the guys will come to me and ask what they should do or, even better, what I think about an idea of their own. I don't pull punches; I tell them it's shit when it's shit, but I tell them *why.* And I also always try to explain how I think they might best reach the goal of their match. Sometimes, when I'm not at a TV taping, out of the blue, I'll text some of the guys when they do something really great, because it's hard to do what they do and to get it right. That positive feedback is important to their confidence and the trust we build with them.

I LEFT MY HEART
IN SAN FRANCISCO

"I faced it all and I stood tall and did it my way"

While my professional career was reaching a zenith, both in the ring and in the office, I was about to experience, to that point, the most devastating loss of my life.

As I've said, as I was growing up, my mother was the only person in my family who truly understood me. We were very close. My mother always had a weak heart. At times, she was very sick and she would have to stay in bed for days. No one was allowed to go in there with her at those times, for as far back as I can remember. Never one to listen, I would sneak into her room and lie beside her, holding her in my arms. I always loved my mother. She spent her entire life taking care of me and my family.

When I was on top in San Francisco, you just couldn't take a day off out of nowhere. But when I got the call that she was very sick and that it would be a good idea if I came back to see her, I didn't hesitate to fly home immediately. When I saw her with the oxygen mask on, I fell to my knees, crying like a baby — I realized how bad things were.

I spent the night at my sister's and then, the following day, my mom didn't need the oxygen anymore.

"Pat, it's because you showed up; she's doing better. It has to be," my sister said.

As I was about to go back to San Francisco, she was back on her feet. I could hold her in my arms and give her a big kiss before going back to work. I wasn't sure if I was ever going to see her again and we were both crying. About a month later, on January 22, 1972, I got the call I feared the most: she was gone. She was only fifty-eight years old. It really hurt me — I felt it in every bone in my body. I can't describe the pain I was in. She was the rock in my life, the one person who was always there for me, who truly understood who I was. We all come from our mothers, and it was as if I had lost a part of myself with her gone.

I was on the other side of the world when I received the news. On top of it all, I needed to work the main event that night, in a cage in Sacramento. I did the goddamn wrestling match, then drove back to San Francisco to catch a red-eye flight that brought me to Montréal just in time for the funeral. I went straight from the airport to the funeral. And then I had to go back to the West Coast almost right away because I was booked. That is how we did things. I had told Roy I couldn't miss the funeral, but I could not afford to stay longer. I was needed at work. It had been eight years since I had brought her to Vegas, and in her bedroom in one of her drawers, the bottle of champagne the flight attendant had given her was still there.

The loss of my mother didn't bring me closer to my dad. And he ended up meeting someone else and beginning a new relationship a few years later. It never became easy between the two of us. Once I came back for the Christmas holidays and stayed with him, but no matter what I tried we were never able to connect.

Let me try to explain just how stubborn he could be. He had an old television set that was in such bad shape that every sound was distorted. You couldn't enjoy anything on that piece of shit. But he would say that the problem wasn't going to last and that the sound would get better. *Right.* I spoke with the rest of the family and asked them how he could watch television like that.

"We tried to get together to buy him a new one, but he would not hear of it because of his damn pride" was what they said.

Anyway, I didn't ask permission; I went to the store and I bought him a television set. When it got there, my dad was huffing and puffing. I told him I'd bought it and that the old one was going in the garbage. I also said, "If you don't want the new one, when I'm gone, you can throw it in the garbage, too." He went quiet and didn't argue. He even finally thanked me.

I wanted to show him that he wasn't the boss of me anymore *and* that he should enjoy life instead of being miserable. For years, that's as good as it ever got between us.

When André the Giant worked in San Francisco, he was happy to meet me because I spoke French. We quickly became friends. When he arrived in town, my friend Davey Rosenberg, a publicist who got me a lot of coverage in the papers, arranged to take pictures of André in a Cadillac with his head sticking out of the sunroof. Of course, that made the papers; Rosenberg was so good at generating that kind of thing.

One time, André had a two-day break before heading back on the road, so I invited him to come to my place to relax.

"You can sleep. Louie is going to cook. It will be great."

That night, after we ate, he went to bed and slept for two days. I actually had to wake him to check if he was still alive.

On another occasion, I went to Las Vegas with him because our television broadcast played there. We were going to see Tom Jones; waiting in line to get in, like everyone else, we stuck out like a sore thumb. I'm not sure if they knew who we were, but they gave us really good seats. Anyway, after the show, we both needed the bathroom. I found a hanger in there and had an idea. I decided to hook it onto the back of his jacket. Without knowing it, André proceeded to walk around the casino with this hanger, complete with a ten-dollar bill attached to it, dangling from his back. I think because no one was used to the surreal sight of someone that big, no one wanted to tell him. Finally, an old lady came up to him and pointed it out, asking what was going on. I was busted — and we had a big laugh about it.

We shared a suite on that trip, with two giant, king-size beds. As we were going back up to our room, this beautiful petite girl came out of the elevator and we almost ran into her.

André said, "*Excusez moi.*"

And she answered right back, "*Excusez moi aussi.*"

They started to speak a little French together, but I was tired and we were drunk and I pushed André into the elevator.

I was asleep for less than half an hour when I heard noises. I got up to find André dressing.

"Where are you going?"

"Don't worry, boss. Half an hour, then I will be right back."

He came back forty-five minutes later with the French lady. I was in my own bed, mind you, but I had a front-row seat for the rest of the evening. It was quite the sight.

During my time in San Francisco, the hippie movement blossomed. It was unbelievable for someone from my humble Montréal background. For a while, it really was all peace and love. And I was known everywhere I went. We traveled to Las Vegas every two weeks and were always treated like stars.

For the first time in my life, I met a lot of other gay people from all walks of life. There were many gay bars and we went to a lot of shows. After a while, I got tired of it. I wanted something . . .

different. I was stuck in a gay-only world. Gay bars, gay restaurants, gay theaters, gay friends: it became too much. I wanted to get away from it. I told Louie we could have people over, but that I didn't want to go out all the time. We decided to move just outside of San Francisco. It was a good life, sure, but I had learned an important lesson: you can have too much of a good thing.

As far as work goes, I had become more popular than I'd ever imagined in my wildest dreams. The territory was lucky to have Davey Rosenberg helping to get us coverage. He'd made a lot of money getting publicity for topless bars in San Francisco — the first city in the U.S. to have that type of establishment. He had great connections in the media. He was a real nice guy and we became good friends and had a lot of fun. One day, he said, "Pat, I have an idea that involves you and the lieutenant governor of California. We are going to have a photo op."

"You gotta be kidding."

"Pat, let me handle this."

And handle it he did. The lieutenant governor, Mervyn M. Dymally, watched wrestling every Wednesday night with his wife, sitting in the front row, with security and everything. He was a big fan. Rosenberg called and spoke with Dymally's secretary. He arranged for me to meet the lieutenant governor of California on the steps of the Capitol.

The lieutenant governor was excited about the arrangements: a 10 a.m. Monday morning meeting. The plan was for him to "give" me one of my jackets, the one I would wear in 1976 to promote the bicentennial of the United States. That's when Rosenberg told me what he really had in mind.

"When he gives it to you, pick him up on your shoulder, and give him an airplane spin. We'll have all the photographers there and we will make the papers for sure."

The next day we made the front page.

We also did that with the mayor of San Francisco, George Moscone, just a week or two before he was killed with Harvey Milk.

In those days, it was really quite rare to get front-page exposure for wrestling. The sports journalists pretty much all hated Roy Shire and the paper barely even published results. Roy was always his charming self with journalists . . . When Rosenberg introduced me to the same journalists, they loved me. Every once in a while, they'd write something good about me. Today, that probably seems like no big deal, but back in those days, it meant something every time.

When you play the good guy, the threat of physical danger from the public disappears, but you've got new responsibilities: you need to be nice to everyone, all the time. And sometimes that's a different kind of pain. It's not always easy. Still, overall, I met more people who had a positive impact in my life than negative.

There was one young fan who was always at the television taping in Sacramento with his mother. One day, I asked them to check on my car and gave him two bucks for their troubles. Later they invited me to eat at their home. I'm still in touch with the kid today — he's no longer a kid and he lives in Las Vegas now. And he still loves wrestling as much as he did back then.

The other pearl I got to know while I was in San Francisco was Dorothy Hopkins. She always seemed to be ringside at the Cow Palace, filming the action with her 8mm camera. Any footage I have from that era is a gift from her. She was a big fan, and she loved me very much. She made me all of my ring jackets. In total, she made twenty-six jackets for me, without me ever asking her for anything. She would just surprise me with them, and I think her payoff was seeing me wear them to the ring. Louie and I became friends with her, and we invited her to some of the parties we had at our house. She really was quite the seamstress.

Not all interactions were quite so positive — crazy shit still happened. One day I was served papers — in a paternity suit. The girl must have been about fourteen when I'd met her for the first time, and she was always at the matches with her mother. They were into my character, big time. They were there early to take pictures and get autographs, and they brought me gifts. That went on for years. Then she disappeared for a while.

By now you know it was quite improbable that I was anyone's father. One night, out of nowhere, they were both back at a show.

"Why are you doing this to me? You know it's not true," I said.

"No, Pat, it's not you," she said, in tears.

I learned that she had a boyfriend, an older guy, who got her pregnant. He turned around and accused me of being the father because he was jealous. The girl still had pictures of me everywhere at home, and he was looking for a way out of his responsibility.

It went to court and everything. The judge asked me only one question: "Did you have a sexual relationship with this girl?"

I answered, "No."

And then he said I should go and wait in his chambers.

I had no idea what was going on, but I was sure it wasn't good. That was way too easy. He came back twenty minutes later telling me that my accuser was full of shit, but that they had to bring the case to court to dismiss it.

"Don't worry, it's not your problem anymore. Come with me to my office across the street." He introduced me to everyone. "This is my man, Pat Patterson. Let's get him a coffee."

Working for Roy wasn't always fun either. Shire was always screaming. He watched every match at every show, so there was always something new for him to yell about. Slowly, however, we developed a kind of trust. What really got us to a good place was that he began discussing match finishes with me, asking how I thought they might be improved. I would take my time and consider it, then I'd offer my two cents. More often than not, he thought my ideas worked.

As time went on, he came to me with ideas more and more frequently. I would help however I could and, in exchange, I was learning psychology from the other side of the curtain.

With that mutual respect, we reached a good place, business-wise. I became much more than just a wrestler even though I didn't have an official role in the office. It also meant that I got mixed up in all of Roy's problems. And that led to the single worst experience of my career.

We had a girl working for us called Miss Wrestling, who went on to become the movie star Adrienne Barbeau. In our show, her job was to look pretty and put a star beside the name of the match's winner. After Adrienne left, she was replaced by another Miss Wrestling. This girl left because she had a falling-out with the promotion and Roy Shire. Seeking revenge, she had a truck full of horse manure dumped behind the studio where we taped our television show. She played dirty and it smelled nasty.

Let's just say Roy had a lot on his mind after all of that transpired. He was in a hotel in Sacramento shortly after that one night and he got into a fight. The guy kicked the shit out of Roy, who was no spring chicken anymore. The police came and Roy had to be helped to his room. Roy's wife called me, crying, "He's at the hotel. He's beat up, he's alone, and he needs help. Please go get him."

I lived south of San Francisco at the time and, from my place, it was a two-hour drive. I got there, helped him get cleaned up, and brought him back to his house. The shit had really hit the fan: he was so out of it we barely talked the whole trip. I had never seen him like that.

The coming week was the annual battle royal at the Cow Palace. It was our biggest show of the year, with wrestlers coming from all over the country. Roy was still out of it and could barely function — he could barely talk, he was a real mess. So I took it upon myself to organize everything and tell the guys how the battle royal was going to go. One of the wrestlers there hated me — and I can never forgive him for what he did that day. Everyone was listening as I gave the match layout, and everyone trusted me, considering Roy was unavailable and I was often in charge.

And then the wrestler who had issues with me stood up and said, "Boys, we don't have to listen to *that* guy," implying that they didn't have to listen to me because I was gay.

"Sit down, you piece of shit. You want to try me?" I said.

It could have become an ugly fight.

Ten guys stood to back me up and things cooled down. All the wrestlers came to me afterward and told me not to worry, that they would keep an eye on him during the battle royal and watch my back.

Peter Maivia even said, "He won't touch you, brother."

I told them I would get him in the battle royal before he tried anything. I'm glad cooler heads prevailed and the match went on without a hitch.

Later he tried to apologize, but that was bullshit.

He even managed to talk one of my best friends, Ricky Hunter, to go along with his crap after the show. I had known Ricky since Portland, and I had brought him to San Francisco. The man even got married in my house. We went years without speaking after that. When I got to Florida years later, his wife finally helped fixed things between us. Later on, in New York, I got him work on television. But again I digress; let's go back to that no-good bastard in San Francisco.

I don't remember who won the damn battle royal, but that's the only time when someone tried to undermine me in wrestling because I was gay and in front of the entire locker room on top of it. Writing about it, it still hurts today. I heard he quit the business not long after that. Which was good for all of us. Years later at the Cauliflower Alley Club in Las Vegas, his wife tried to patch things up, telling me he was sorry. I told her that I could never forgive him.

You can curse me all you want, but don't ever hold that against me. I have been in charge for years, and you develop a thick skin in this business. But you never get used to being belittled for who you are, especially not in front of the dressing room. I wanted to fight and, I am not ashamed to say it, I felt like I could have killed him. I just saw red that day: it could happen in other places but not in my world. In my world, I was Pat Patterson — and I knew our business; being gay didn't matter. I can't fully explain it, but that was the most hurtful thing to ever happen to me in wrestling and I will never fully recover from the shame and pain of that day. I still have the scar, and that's why I don't want to give him any notoriety by naming him.

Roy finally got back on his feet. He ran a big territory and he did it all by himself from a small home office. I had his trust. And today that means more to me than it probably did back then. After a while, he decided to finally take a vacation, and he asked me to handle the wrestlers' payoff. He put all their names and the amount they were due on a sheet, and then he wrote me a check for the total amount. I was to deposit the check and then write checks for each individual from my own account — that's how much he trusted me. It went so well that we kept doing that until I left the territory. He was a tough man, but for some reason he liked me. If he didn't, there was no way I could have lasted fourteen years working for him. In the end I left of my own accord. I had just had enough — fourteen years wrestling main events in the same territory, with the same crowd sitting in the same first five rows in every city . . . You can't imagine the pressure I felt trying to find something new to do the next week to keep them coming back. They had seen me do everything twice, as both a good guy and a bad guy. Eventually, you start questioning yourself about everything. It had stopped being fun.

The business itself was also getting a bit messy at the end. Since our television show had become so strong, Roy got tired of giving a cut to the local promoters who barely did anything to promote the shows. Shire owned all the rings in every town, except for a few where he was partnered with a local promoter. One guy actually cut the ring in half and gave Roy his share when they split up. Others were mad because Shire would not let us work for them anymore. Some of them were mad because they felt they'd helped Roy establish the territory. As always, Roy Shire could really make your life miserable.

Despite all of this, toward the end of my run in San Francisco, Louie and I tried to buy into the territory, but Roy would not sell or even accept us as partners. I had been working so hard for him without getting much of anything for all the creative work and time I put into it. I wanted a piece of the action. By that point, I handled most of the shows on the road and Roy stayed home. So, I eventually told him that I had to leave. He finally did give me a town as a way of trying to keep me — and he said I could do what I wanted with the show, that I had free rein. But there was a local promoter already involved there and, by the time he had taken his share, there wasn't much money left for me — certainly not enough to compensate me for all the work I had been doing for years. Hindsight being 20/20, buying into the territory would have been a bad investment. But just to show you how difficult Roy could be, even with me, consider this: one time I wanted to do a cage match in my town, and Roy wanted me to rent my own truck to come and pick up the cage at his place. And then he charged me for using his cage . . . That did it; I needed to go. I never received anything for all the behind-the-scenes work I did; I was never paid for anything except for my wrestling matches. And, in truth, I also liked many of those local promoters he was warring with. They would all ask me what was wrong with Roy. I told them they already knew the answer: Shire was cheap.

I couldn't do anything for them, and I couldn't do anything for Roy when he was pissed at them. When times were tougher, he was happy to have those guys working with him, but when things got easier, well, he didn't appreciate everyone who had helped get him where he was.

The last singles match I appeared in for Roy Shire was a loser-leaves-town gimmick against Alexis Smirnoff, a kid from Montréal playing a Russian. I dropped the championship, and that was it. I had done everything, and I desperately needed an incentive to stay. If none was coming, so be it. My years in San Francisco were some of the best of my life and of my career. I did get an education with Roy and the foundation of the career I had after I left the ring was laid in San Francisco.

I left for Florida to work for Eddie Graham, another wrestling genius. But I wasn't just a wrestler there: with Johnny Valentine, I became a producer for the territory. I needed to go, and yes it took me a little while to find myself again . . . But first, if you have not jumped ahead already, the Ray Stevens chapter is finally next.

Enjoy. We'll travel to Florida soon enough.

THE BLOND BOMBERS

"I did what I had to do and saw it through without exemption"

Only Ray Stevens and I knew the whole truth of what am I about to tell you. I'm going to let you in on the special moments and secrets we shared, and about our deep friendship.

What do I mean?

No, I did *not* have sex with Ray Stevens . . . Well, OK, not exactly.

Ray Stevens was in Australia when I first arrived in San Francisco in January 1965, so we weren't paired up until he returned. Roy Shire had me dye my hair blond to match Ray's platinum locks and I became his new tag-team partner. Don Manoukian, a former Oakland Raiders football player, had been Ray's partner. He was a great guy and one hell of a performer himself, but he was retiring — my timing could not have been better.

The match was scheduled for April 17, 1965: Roy Shire brought in Dick Beyer, as The Destroyer, and his tag-team partner, Billy Red Lyons, up from Los Angeles. Ray and I were facing the West Coast World Tag-Team Champions, and I knew things could go either way. Roy had never told me that we would become the champions, and

I felt I still needed to prove myself every night and deliver on what I had promised him on my first day. But the fact was, because we were booked in a championship match, I knew there was a chance. The only problem was I was so sick I almost couldn't get out of bed. Louie wanted me to stay home and even called in a doctor — he was that worried. The doctor said he wanted me to stay in bed for the next three days — *no buts*, and no wrestling for the championship. If I had listened to him, there is no telling the opportunity I might have missed, or how the path of my career might have been altered. Louie was furious with me, but he said he'd rather drive me to the arena and take care of me, rather than worrying about me getting there by myself. He probably didn't really expect anything different — he knew that was how the business went. If I missed that night, who knew would happen to Ray and me when I was better? I knew I *had* to be there, and ultimately he respected that. And I was right. That night, we became the tag-team champions for the first time. Louie knew how I was and that the business came first. The truth is, Louie never really got involved in any decision I made in relation to wrestling. He trusted me and I truly appreciated that. After the win, everything fell into place professionally for Ray and me.

In my book, I would put Roy Shire, Eddie Graham, and Dory Funk Sr. on my short list of wrestling geniuses. There are many other good painters out there, don't get me wrong, but not everyone can be a Picasso. But Ray Stevens, as far as wrestling performance goes, also has a place on that short list. He got it right, and got it right all the time. And it seemed like everything came to him naturally, that he never had to struggle to learn anything. Shawn Michaels might be the best comparison I can give to help you understand how good Ray Stevens was. Ray was a prodigy. Now, if you said that to his face he would probably tell you that you were full of shit and that he wished he would have worked openers instead of main events, so he could have more time to chase women and drink beer . . . Do you want even more proof of his talent? Before I got to the territory, he won the award for Most Hated Wrestler in the Bay Area. But what's truly remarkable is that he also won Most Popular Wrestler for the same year. Ray was unique — just like me.

And what a great friend Ray became. Naturally, we spent a lot of time together when we were on the road, and from the start, we had a lot of fun. But he almost got me killed in the ring once. It was a three-man tag elimination match: Stevens and me, with Freddie Blassie as our partner, at the Cow Palace. On TV, the three of us explained in detail what we were going to do to the fans' favorites. As the match wore on, we lost Fred. But as we had predicted on TV, in the end Ray and I, two-on-one, were running roughshod over crowd-favorite Pepper Gomez — his partners had already been eliminated. We beat the goddamn hell out of him. It was so intense that the fans wanted to jump in to help defend Pepper against our onslaught. Finally, unbelievably, they came out of the crowd — there must have been more than fifty fans in the ring with us. I was sure I was going to die   I was in the middle of a goddamn riot and I could not get out of the ring. Dozens of cops had to be called in just so they could "safely" get us back to the dressing room.

The cops encircled us and said they were going to bring us to the back one at a time. I told Ray to go first. As the police were pushing people out of their way, the angry mob pushed back. Suddenly I saw Ray's blond head disappear into the crowd. It was terrifying, and I was sure something had happened to him. But then he popped up again and seemed to make it to the back. At that moment, the crowd turned all their attention on me. I was sure I was done.

Even with the police escort, I almost never made it to the dressing room door. Someone hit me over the head with a bottle and I was covered in blood, and I was sure it was my last day on earth. I actually don't remember the moment I realized I was safely back in the dressing room, and all I could say, over and over again, was "I can't believe I'm alive."

Lying on the floor and trying to stop the bleeding, my only thought was how lucky I was. Ray was mad but, just like me, glad to be alive. For two guys who really just wanted to have fun, it was no laughing matter.

That Cow Palace was one of the most dangerous buildings in the country back then. (And even today you need to be careful when you wrestle in San Francisco. Chris Jericho was hit on the head by a D battery thrown from the crowd just a few years ago.) When the fans rioted, we had to wait two hours before we could even leave the building. The lynch mob was still waiting for us. Everybody was scared, even Ray. And scaring Ray was no easy feat.

There were a few times when issues like that turned into a good laugh. One night in Eureka, California, just before the show began the chief of police came to the dressing room and asked to speak to the person in charge. I pointed to Roy, and he started to explain there was a bomb threat. He told us there were two options: evacuate everybody and cancel the show, or sign a waiver saying Roy was responsible if something happened.

Roy picked number two, in case you were wondering. Everyone was nervous, and the main event pitted Ray and me against Mr. Fuji and Mr. Saito. When we made our entrance, the only thing in our mind was that a main event was about to blow us all to kingdom come. Before the opening bell, as the referee gave us instructions, we heard a *pow!* We all bolted from the ring, fearing for our lives.

Do you know what had happened?

A kid at ringside had stomped on a paper cup. The tension broke and I think all of us were trying to hide our laughter for the rest of the match.

Not everything was as tense as that, of course. Once a month, we would go to Reno and Lake Tahoe to visit the casinos and see some shows. For three years, we also worked Las Vegas and enjoyed Sin City on a monthly basis. It was fun: we were both well known and the pit boss would get us into all the shows for free, so they could claim to have celebrities in attendance. We had front-row seats and complimentary champagne whenever we wanted. Ray enjoyed that even more than I did. We saw all the greats: Frank Sinatra, Sammy Davis Jr., Tom Jones, Liberace . . .

I'm a smoker, and before you start admonishing me, I know it's a fucking bad habit. Vince keeps telling me that all the time. But it's all Ray Stevens's fault: he's the one who got me to try this shit. I was drunk one night and he pressured me, laughing because I was coughing and having a hard time. After a while, I stopped coughing but I never stopped smoking. There's no doubt I picked up this vice hanging with Ray Stevens.

But not everything we did was bad for me. In a Reno club one night, two gorgeous ladies came over to talk to us. We were sure they recognized us. They told us we were handsome and that they needed two volunteers to get their hair colored on stage. Of course we said yes — I always loved to be on stage. People in the audience recognized us and we got a big reaction. And we got our hair dyed for free! Wrestlers and their freebies . . .

Even if I was stuck with him twenty-four hours a day, Ray was a blast to be around. In his mind, he was always nineteen. And he was always either a kid at a party, on a motorcycle, fishing, horseracing, hunting, in a wrestling ring . . . or in bed with a woman. He was always ready to try something new, and he could never get enough of the ladies.

Years later, when I was a good guy and facing Ray, someone in the crowd yelled, "Stevens, you queer."

Under his breath, Ray said to me, "If they only knew."

It took everything we had not to laugh because everyone in the match *but* Ray —the referee, the ring announcer, and me — *was* gay.

On another occasion, in a small town just outside of San Francisco, somebody shouted something similar and Ray just couldn't keep it together. He actually fell to his knees laughing. Those were the days: people called us queer just because of our dyed blond hair.

As you can see, Ray knew everything about me. And the fact that I was gay did not prevent him from asking me to help him in getting women into his bed. We went to a party once at the home of Ray's new neighbors. He insisted I come because he wanted to get the woman into bed and he needed someone to distract the husband. Let's just say Ray almost always got what he wanted. In a strange turn of events, the husband showed up one day . . . to see me. I always wondered if Ray knew, or if it was just his luck rubbing off on me.

I remember going to Ray's place to pick him up. It was 2 p.m., the time we'd agreed upon, but he was nowhere to be found. I asked his wife, and of course she said he was still in bed. Damn it, we had to leave right away. I had to go into his room and start yelling at my partner, who was unconscious with the mother of all hangovers.

"Come on, Ray, we have to get going."

He began mumbling, and that's the only way I knew he was alive. But I could not understand anything he was saying, and he was definitely not moving. I went to his kitchen to make coffee, hoping he would start getting dressed as I had asked. When I returned, he was still in bed, snoring.

"Come on, Ray, get out of bed."

Finally, he slowly started to come out of his coma and move towards the edge of the bed. I went back to the kitchen, hoping this time he would start to get dressed. When I didn't hear any other sounds from the bedroom, I started to worry. When I went back to check on him, he was standing naked in the closet, keeping himself steady by holding onto the closet rod with both hands. There was a woman's shoe right in front of him. I was puzzled and didn't say a word. What in the hell was he trying to do?

He was attempting to position the shoe with his feet, trying to get it perfectly in front of him, and he was obviously struggling in his still half-drunk condition. Finally, he got it. And then he started to piss. In the shoe. In his own closet.

I went straight back down to the kitchen to make sure his wife was not coming up. If she had, we would have never left — she would have killed him. Ultimately, I was able to get a half-dressed Ray Stevens into the car, so we could leave for the show. By the time it was bell time, he performed as brilliantly as usual, as if nothing had happened. Ray Stevens was never worried about anything in the ring.

I had that ability as well. No matter what we did the night before, I could always go in a match. Ray had been a star in San Francisco long before me, but he was much more a playboy than a business-man. He was never interested in the inner workings of our industry, or in discussing what we should do in a main event with Roy or, later on in Minnesota, with Verne Gagne. He didn't stress and he was always confident he could play everything by ear.

"Tell me what you want and I'll just do it," he would say.

He had an opinion, sure, but as long as things made sense, he was fine. He figured things out in the ring.

I went hunting with Ray Stevens once — once and only once. We were hunting for mountain lions in California, if you can believe it. We were out all goddamn night and we didn't see a thing. That didn't faze him at all — while I am still pissed about it. Ray never did anything without investing himself 100% — when he got into rodeos, for example, what did you think he did? He bought a horse, with the big truck and trailer and everything you need to take a horse everywhere. He didn't get out with the animal much, mind you, but he had everything. He got injured doing that kind of stuff, too. When he got into motorcycles, he got into a wreck and had to miss a lot of action for quite a while after his accident. If something like that happened to anyone else, Roy Shire would have fired him, no questions asked. Roy's business, and all the wrestlers' welfare, depended on us drawing crowds to the main event. And Ray let everyone down. Ultimately, Roy was right, you can't afford to let the talent take unnecessary risks. Today, someone like John Cena is too busy — he doesn't have time to get into that kind of nonsense; hell, he barely has time to go to the restroom.

That doesn't mean Roy didn't ask us to do crazy things when it benefited him. Roy had a ranch, and when the bulls reached a certain age, most needed to be castrated to make sure the females bred only with the best stock. Roy, Ray, and I would get on horses to round up the cattle. Roy would always want us to go easy because if we scared them, it would be impossible to round them up for at least a week. One time, we screwed up and they all but disappeared for days. Roy was so mad. It was funny, and Ray was the one laughing the loudest.

Anyway, we had to restrain the bulls before leading them through a cattle chute. It was gross: you have to cut a bull's scrotum, pull on its balls, and cut them out. As someone would do that, I would stand on top of the bull, holding its tail up, making sure it couldn't move any part of its body. Once we were done, up came the next bull. I eventually wound up doing the actual cutting. Roy would invite us for dinner afterward. At first, Louie thought we were barbarians, but he ended up helping too and he liked it. The fact that Ray had him drink a few vodkas first probably helped change his mind. Of course, Roy had experts there helping us, and they made sure we never injured ourselves despite the danger. I wonder if he would have fired us if we did . . . And who would have believed that the little Clermont kid with girls' skates would end up neutering bulls as cowboy Pat Patterson?

Whether it was skiing, rodeo, or motorcycle accidents, or whether you were injured in the ring, it didn't matter — back then you were on your own with no money coming in. But that was fine with Ray Stevens: never looking ahead, always living in the moment. I had more fun in and out of the ring with him than with anyone else. It was a goddamned unbelievable time. Some guys don't get along this well with their tag-team partner — one guy wants his wife around all the time, another doesn't want to go to the bar, another gets up too early on road trips. But with Ray, it was all a picnic.

"Whatever you want to do, Pat," he would say.

I know I just said as much, didn't I? It doesn't matter, I'll say it again because it was true. We were such a good match; there was no ego, no bullshit from either of us. We did our job and we loved it. We were fucking good, that's it.

One time, in Milwaukee, the promoter paid Ray with a $6,000 check. He didn't want to waste time going to the bank, so he asked the guy if he could exchange it for cash from the night's box office.

The promoter came back with a bag stuffed with $6,000. He insisted that Ray count it, because he didn't want to have any disagreement in the future.

Ray sat there for hours, trying to count the whole thing. Each time he got going, someone would come in to talk to him and he could never remember where he was. So he started all over again. I even tried to help him so we could get out of there, but he said no. Don't worry, he told me, I'll do it. After a while, he grew frustrated and grabbed up all the money from the table, stuffed it back into the bag, and said, "The hell with it, six thousand."

That was it for him; it was time to spend that money.

When we finally began the program that pitted me against Ray, people were ready for it. We went weeks with a simple story that teased the idea of "Who was going to be the first to break the rules?" On television, the host would ask the fans, the wrestlers, the referees, and even the ring announcer what they thought. Everyone was invested in our rivalry — it just needed time to brew. Even if it was simple, it was perfect. We had years of matches teaming together to build on. Roy was so good at that — he could build a good story on little details. Some people don't realize that you need to *make* a team before breaking them up. And that takes time. As in any good movie or story, there needs to be an emotional investment.

The only bad thing about it was that when we started our rivalry, we had to stop hanging out. Roy Shire would fire you if you crossed that line, and we tried to never break that rule. We loved the business too much.

For one of our matches, he came to the ring wearing boxing headgear. Ray had built it up real good during his interviews, saying that he had a surprise for me. When he unveiled it in the ring, people went crazy. I was mad, saying how unfair this was because I couldn't use my loaded mask to head-butt him, which was my gimmick as the bad guy. During that match, nothing I could do would hurt him, so I ripped off his headgear in frustration. It was a simple concept but it worked. Roy had input in these matches, too, and we drew a lot of money. More importantly, we had fun.

Today, when I think about teaming with Ray, I get choked up. He was such a great guy and he was already a name by the time we partnered. He didn't have to accept me as an equal, or even like me, but he helped me so much and we became the best of friends. He could have said that he didn't want to be paired up with "that queer" and that would have been it for me in San Francisco. (Though I'm sure he thought teaming with a gay man meant all the more women for him.) I was very fortunate that we made one hell of a team. And that we also clicked fighting each other. People just loved seeing us in the ring together, no matter what we were doing. That doesn't mean Ray, that crazy bastard, treated me differently from anybody else.

We were wrestling in Hawaii once when a wrestler by the name of Handsome Johnny Barend got married in the ring. I was in the shower just when the bride was passing by our dressing room and I wanted to catch a peek. I was covered in soap and naked as she came by the door and that's when Bill Watts and Ray Stevens pushed me out of the dressing room. I slipped right on my ass, buck naked, in front of Handsome Johnny's bride.

She was so impressed she almost canceled the wedding.

And those two assholes were killing themselves laughing at me. That's the kind of joke *I* could pull, but when I was the victim, I guess I got a little mad. But in the end, I could laugh about it.

The United States Championship we fought over in San Francisco is the only memento, the only thing from my career I would really like to own — that's how much that time and that territory meant to me. And though I need that championship like I need another hole in my head, and I don't know if I would even display it, I still want it. That championship is special to me: it's not about the wrestling, it brings me back to my life in San Francisco, teaming with Ray and living happily ever after with Louie . . .

Ray Stevens was more than my partner — we would have gone through hell for each other, and we did. Photo courtesy of *Pro Wrestling Illustrated*.

Oh yeah, I almost forgot: I didn't tell you about me and Ray sleeping together. Kind of.

A couple of times, he asked me to join him and a girl, because the girl wanted to be with the both of us. I wanted to be a good pal, so I never said no. I even tried to get into it at first. But I would wind up letting them finish their thing and then get out of there. Louie never knew, even though we were free to do what we wanted. I figured you only live once . . . And while Ray Stevens was around . . .

I remember this mother and daughter duo who used to come see us wrestle. (Yes, she was way older than eighteen.) They would wait for us, take pictures, and ask for autographs. They came around for months and Ray was infatuated with the daughter. Each time we saw them, he would not stop talking about how hot she was. So one night after the matches, Ray said, "Pat, come back with me. We'll take my truck and we'll stop by some friends of mine. They have food and beers for us."

You know how it goes, it sounded good on paper: free food and booze. Still, I didn't want us to stay too long. We had a long road trip ahead of us.

When we get there, Ray's friends were the mother and daughter. And yes, I cursed his good name a little. He pleaded with me to play along. I knew what he had in mind and I also knew my only option was to follow his lead. I had to be a good friend.

By 2 a.m., we were having fun, eating sandwiches and drinking beer. We were a little drunk when Ray and the daughter snuck off to her room. That's when the mother kidnapped me, dragged me to her room, and had her way with me.

You could never say no to Ray Stevens; he would convince you that jumping into a fiery pit was the best idea in the world. How many of you have good friends like that? I admit I did this kind of thing a few times for Ray, and on the road Stevens would even pick up a girl here and there and get her to give me a blow job. When he would ask me how it was, I would tell him, "I certainly could have given her lessons."

Ray was probably happier about conning me into sleeping with these girls than sleeping with them himself. He would brag to the other wrestlers about it and we would all laugh. "Me and Pat, we made love to the most incredible woman together last night. She was the hottest . . ." When Ray asked, I would take one for the team. And yet one time I almost had my revenge.

It was years later, in Milwaukee, when we were wrestling for the American Wrestling Association. We were on last, and the snowstorm of the century was raging outside. Because of the weather, everyone left as soon as they were done with their match. Ray said, "Let's take our time. The hell with it. We can't get out of here anyway."

We had two cases of beer with us, so we started to talk and drink. A few hours later, it was still snowing. We had our bags to carry, no more beer, and we were drunk. No one was left in the building. But Ray always had brilliant ideas. There was a bar a block away. We could see its lights on. It seemed like the only place that was open in the entire city. We decided to walk there through what must have been three feet of snow, with our bags on our shoulders. Brilliant ideas, as I said. We finally made it to the bar, and it was empty except for four girls. We sat, ordered a round of drinks, and tried to call a cab. While we waited, and after a few more drinks, Ray asked, "Pat, how come the broads are so large in this place?"

I kept avoiding an answer, but as we drank, he kept asking. Finally, I said to him with my most serious face, "Ray, they're all drag queens. You want to take one for the team *for me* tonight?"

We laughed hysterically once again.

By the time Ray got to work for WWE, I'd already had my main-event run, so it wasn't the same. New York was never really a territory based around tag teams. I think we had our last matches as a team in 1982 in the Carolinas, and then got together for a quick tour back in the AWA later that year. I had started to work behind the scenes in New York by then, and I was also a babyface.

We didn't see nearly enough of each other after he left WWE. On April 5, 1995, years after he stopped wrestling, the cities of both San Francisco and Oakland jointly declared it Ray Stevens Day in the Bay Area. Incredible, isn't it?

Ray died in 1996 from a

Believe me, Ray rarely looked that calm when we were together. We had a lot of fun. Photo courtesy of Linda Boucher.

heart attack. He was only sixty years old. I could not believe he had passed away, even though Ray was always careless about his health. Eventually it caught up to him: I heard he drank and smoked until his very last day.

Ray was Ray.

I didn't go to his funeral. If I had to do it all over again, I would have. I've told you how it is — and in '96, I was working a full-time schedule for WWE. And the funeral was held in San Francisco, at the other end of the country, thousands of miles from my home in Connecticut. In wrestling, you feel obligated to your job and you put the work before friendship. It's one of the real regrets I have in my life, not attending Ray's funeral. Other than my mother and Louie, knowing that he was not out there anymore was probably one of the hardest things I've ever had to accept.

Everyone loved Ray Stevens. And I will always remember what he used to say when I would call bullshit on one of his stories: "If a story is worth telling, it's worth coloring, Pat." Let me tell you, I didn't need a lot of coloring when I worked and traveled with Ray. If you don't believe me, just ask Ric Flair, who showed him how to have fun after work.

Late at night, when we worked together, anyone around us could hear him laughing through the walls of the hotel. You knew he was having a good time. Today, when I hear laughter on the road, I like to pretend Ray is right there, too, having fun. He was the type of guy who could leave to get a loaf of bread for his wife and come back two days later.

Maybe he's still out there, just getting bread.

9

LOOKING FOR MYSELF IN FLORIDA AND MINNEAPOLIS

"I've had my fill, my share of losing"

The Shire territory had been good for me financially, and I always took care of my money. I was at home in my own bed almost every night and I was working on top most of the time. Everybody wanted to work the territory, but it was time to move on. When the time came to leave San Francisco in 1977, we had this great place, close to downtown. Louie had his barbershop business and we were making money. You can't ask for anything more than that, right? Without hesitation, when I told Louie I was going to work in Florida, he said, "Let's go." I was a lucky man. Jim Barnett hired me to be in charge of the Florida territory, along with Johnny Valentine. Florida was a small territory with big names — and all of those big names lived there full-time. Valentine was really old school. Our philosophies were so different that it was no fun, and I decided I didn't want to be in charge. I told the promoter, Eddie Graham, that I was just going to be a wrestler. Valentine wanted to turn everything upside down, to get rid of the Brisco brothers and Dusty Rhodes. Jack and Gerald

Brisco were suddenly booked in opening matches and the blame was put on me. Go see Valentine, I told them.

Still, there were great things about that time. I became good friends with Dusty, the Briscos, and everyone there.

When I was in San Francisco, I was always billed as being from Montréal. But when I got to Florida, they started to say I was from San Francisco. I would do interviews where I would explain how California was the best state in the Union. I would go on and on to explain that Californian fruits were so much better, juicer and tastier than the fruits in Florida. I would have the wrestlers rolling on the floor laughing in the dressing room, while I was cutting those promos. I had a fruit basket on my jacket with the lettering "California fruits." I was always able to poke fun at myself — that's why I never had any issues while with WWE when my friend Gorilla Monsoon or others would poke fun at me while doing commentary. I was in on the laugh from the beginning.

I met the young Terry Bollea for the first time while he was playing in a band in a Florida bar where wrestlers hung out. He was tall and skinny. On the very first day he came in for wrestling training, I happened to be at the gym. The whole office was playing jokes on the man who would become Hulk Hogan, and Hogan himself says that I was the only one who actually taught him anything that day. I wish I could say I saw right away that he was going to become the biggest star in the world. But that would be lying — and I'm not the kind of person who'd blow smoke up your ass.

Stop laughing, it's true.

I was honestly just trying to be nice to the kid. In Florida, if you wanted to be a wrestler, they would make you pay for it by stretching and hurting you. They knew him from the bar scene, so they were ribbing him more than hurting him, but I didn't see the point in not helping him. I didn't know he was going to be a star, I just wanted to be helpful. Hell, I wish I knew. Gerald Brisco helped him a lot later on, too. I rode with him to his first match. We ribbed him.

"You haven't seen anything yet, kid. If you want to get initiated in the business, you need to give a blow job to one of the wrestlers."

We drove him crazy, the poor bastard. He didn't come back with us. But we were just kidding. This was dressing room humor, and even the straight guys were in on it. We laughed about that all night wondering how he got home. I think he even laughs about it in his second book. (I know, everyone wrote a book before I got around to it.)

The drive from West Palm Beach to Tampa is almost three and a half hours. At night, you can't see anything anywhere. I'm riding with goddamn Terry Funk once when he said, "Stop the car, Pat. There's a cornfield. We are going to steal some corn. Open the trunk; come and help."

It was so dark that without even realizing it, I walked straight into the goddamn mud. I was almost up to my knees and cursing the name of Terry Funk, but we filled the trunk with corn. I was filthy. Funk laughed about it for the rest of the ride; he'd got me good.

Another time on the same road, a cop pulled me over. The cop was nice. "You're Pat Patterson. I watch you guys on television. You guys are good. Where did you work tonight?"

"West Palm Beach, sir," I said politely.

"Are any other wrestlers coming this way?"

"Yeah, the Brisco brothers must be just a few minutes behind me. Why don't you pull them over, too? Scare them a little?"

What I didn't know was that the Briscos were drinking beer on the way home.

When they heard the sirens, they went crazy trying to get rid of the evidence. Finally, the cop came to talk with them: "Patterson told me to stop you."

Jesus Christ, I'm still laughing.

I really don't like flying in small planes, but sometimes you need to, just to save time. I flew to Tallahassee with Eddie Graham in his personal plane once, and even though he only had one good eye, he was the pilot. His son Mike Graham was sitting up front, and Eddie kept asking him to read the instruments. I could not wait for them to land that thing. I never ever flew in his plane again.

Getting to Miami was a long, godforsaken trip. One time, a few wrestlers decided to rent a small plane and split the cost to get home early. Sometimes, we had good ideas like that . . . I was in the back, having fun, when the pilot said, "I think we have a problem, guys. The wheels aren't coming down."

"What?"

He kept repeating the same thing. "The wheels aren't coming down."

He called the tower and they confirmed visually that only two out of three wheels were deployed.

"What are we going to do?" I said.

"We sure as hell can't stay up here all night," he said.

He landed that plane, nose tilted up, on only two wheels.

After that, no more small planes in Florida for me.

I was in Florida for less than a year. When working with Valentine didn't pan out, there wasn't much left for me to accomplish. What was I going to do next? I had done everything at least once in the wrestling business. I was probably a little burned out, too, and I was seriously thinking about retiring. I was only thirty-six years old.

And then Verne Gagne called me to bring me to Minneapolis for the AWA. The conversation went a little like this:

"Do you have blond hair?"

"Yes, why?"

"I don't want blonds; I got too many."

Like he didn't know I'd had blond hair for the past fifteen years.

"Well, if you don't want blond hair, then you don't want Pat Patterson. I'm not coming."

"Do you do interviews?"

"What the hell do you think I have been doing for the past fifteen years?"

"I will think about it."

"Think fast because I will be booked someplace else."

He gave me a start date before we ended the conversation.

I had some good times in Minneapolis. There was lots of travel there, too, and lots of small plane trips in bad weather. We called the AWA plane *Suicide 1*, and for good reason. That tin can scared the shit out of me every time I stepped inside. We were in Chicago one time when I told the pilot I was going to sit up front with him. The plane could only accommodate eight passengers and somehow I felt better beside the pilot. I remember a big 747 right in front of us before we took off. At 5,000 feet, I saw oil leaking from our wing.

The pilot said, "Shit, they didn't tighten it enough. We'll have to go back and make an emergency landing."

I was scared out of my mind. I had already had one emergency landing, in Florida, and statistically you are not supposed to get more than one of those in your life. That pilot was just dangerous: the plane would have inches of ice on its wings before he'd finally decide we needed to land. Guys would take tranquilizers just to sleep through trips with him in that death trap. Let me tell you, Chicago to Winnipeg is a long goddamn flight.

I wrestled everyone in the AWA: Gagne, Dick the Bruiser, The Crusher, and even Mad Dog. It was fun to be with Maurice once again. This time, I could help him by taking care of him when we fought each other.

I also hooked up with Ray Stevens as a tag team once again. We had another main-event run and a great time as usual. But it was damned cold all the time, and after living in California and Florida for so long, winter seemed even worse than it had been growing up in Montréal.

Lord Alfred Hayes was another good friend, and we were able to reconnect in the AWA. I actually tried to teach him how to ski. It was not going well: he took his first fall as we were coming off the chairlift. I was a patient, persistent teacher, however, and he managed a couple of decent runs before he lost control and disappeared into the woods. I had to take my skis off to go looking for him. When I found him, he was covered in snow just a few yards away from a cliff. I asked him what happened and he said, with his distinctive British accent, "Well, Patrick, I was totally out of control."

I had a lot of fun playing golf with Hayes as well, both in Minnesota and later in New York. The first time we played, he didn't know how to golf, though he made me believe he did.

"What are you going to use?" I asked on the first hole.

"I'm going with my trusty 7-iron." And then he hit the ball straight into the woods.

Lord Alfred was always in character. When I would miss the cup by an inch, he would say, "What a noble effort."

We laughed a lot together.

I helped Alfred get into New York. I talked to Vince about him, and he loved Lord Alfred's promos right away. He became a fixture on *Tuesday Night Titans*, co-hosting with Vince. The show is available on WWE Network now, if you are curious.

By the time we got to Minneapolis, Louie had sold the barbershop in San Francisco and decided to stay home and stop working.

We were well-off and it was a lot of work to take care of our home life. We enjoyed ourselves, and had a good social life as well. Louie would hang out with the wrestlers' wives while we were on the road. Nick Bockwinkel, Mad Dog, and Ray Stevens made sure that we came into the territory with a great reputation. Louie was such a bright man and everyone in the AWA loved him. We would hang out with all the straight couples, guys like Bockwinkel, Jim Brunzell, and Greg Gagne — even if his dad, Verne, was just like Roy Shire to begin with. Louie and I would eat at their places and hang out with their children just like any other couple. Verne Gagne couldn't stand gay people when I first got there, but as time went by he became curious and wanted to meet Louie. He was hearing all these incredible stories about him and the great meals Louie would cook. So he finally mustered the courage to ask, "When am I going to taste Louie's cuisine for myself?"

I told him he was more than welcome to come over.

"No, I want you guys to come to my place — let's cook a big meal for all the wrestlers."

Louie said yes and when he began cooking, he actually kicked Verne out of his own kitchen, because he tried to stick his nose in Louie's meal. "It's my kitchen now, get out." That's how Louie was.

Sometimes we'd get back from a show late and Greg Gagne would come home with me to shoot the shit with Louie and hang out. Louie made him laugh. He told him once, "I don't know if listening to your philosophy is doing me any good or if you're confusing me." We all laughed.

I was in Minneapolis for the better part of the next two years and continued to do occasional shots for Verne for a few years after that.

I left Minneapolis because Ray and I were almost done our run as a tag team. I wanted to know what Verne had planned for us . . . Ray wouldn't bother himself with that shit, but I needed to know. I went to Verne's office by myself to talk about the next six to twelve months: I was happy; I was making good money. But I wanted to know what was next. Verne's answer was "I don't reveal my secrets."

"OK," I said. "Then I won't tell you mine."

That upset him, and he told me that I wasn't being fair. I countered that he was the one being unfair. If he wouldn't reveal his plans for me, I wouldn't reveal what I had planned for myself.

It was difficult; I had built a special relationship with Roy over the years, and I would have loved to do the same with Verne. But that just wasn't his style. I had arrived at a crossroads: I could no longer be satisfied just being a wrestler.

I always appreciated learning new things, but there was nothing left for me to learn after nearly two years in Minnesota. Whatever feelings I had about retiring were gone, too. I wanted more, and I wanted something new. I think that's why being a wrestler and traveling all over the world was the perfect career for me. There is always something new waiting for you, and this time it was waiting for me in the Big Apple.

My secret was that I had an offer on the table to go to New York to work for Vince McMahon Sr.

NEW YORK! NEW YORK!

"Yes, there were times, I'm sure you knew, when I bit off more than I could chew"

As I've said, I craved a new challenge. Mike LeBell, the Los Angeles promoter, was good friends with Vince McMahon Sr. He suggested I contact Vince. I called and when Vince explained his plan for me I told him I would be there . . . *tomorrow.*

"No, no," he said. "I don't want any heat. Just wait. I will give you a date when I've talked it over with Verne."

I had met Vince Sr. for the first time a few years earlier in Las Vegas. Roy Shire was never a member of the National Wrestling Alliance but, as a courtesy, every year he was invited to attend their annual general meeting. They were hoping he would change his mind and join them. At very least, it kept relationships good for everyone. One year, Roy brought me with him. But because having a top talent sitting with all those promoters in "important" meetings was awkward, I ended up befriending Vince's wife, Juanita.

I was all dressed up and waiting for the last meeting of the day to end when I finally said, "We're not going to wait on them forever. Let's go to the bar and have some cocktails."

The promoters' wives all thought it was a fabulous idea. So we went to the bar and had a blast. I guess I was charming, and I was definitely making them laugh. I don't know why, but I was always very popular with the ladies. Juanita never got involved with the wrestling business, but I was the exception to the rule. She spoke the world of me to Vince Sr.

When he decided to bring me in a few years later, he planned for me to wrestle Bob Backlund for the World Heavyweight Championship. That was a new and exciting platform: to be in the main event on the grandest stage of them all. Guys who were my size didn't usually come to New York to challenge for the championship. As I said, I was not contacted directly. Back then, they were very cautious about things like that. That's something that would change when Vince Jr. took over — but that's a story for later.

When I first showed up in New York, Vince Sr. asked his right-hand man, Arnold Skaaland, to take care of me and show me around his territory. When André the Giant was on the same card, we traveled together. Talk about getting drunk — we were quite the trio. Arnold could really hold his liquor and even go toe-to-toe with André. He was one of the few who could honestly say that. Arnold could also find a place to buy beer in any town, any day, any time. One time, we drove up to a house in the middle of nowhere and I was sure we were just dropping in on a friend. No, he knew we could buy beers there. Those were the days: he had been in the territory for years, yet I was still impressed. I had been in San Francisco for close to fifteen years and I could not have done the same thing. Later on I did my best to take care of Skaaland, who was always afraid of being kicked to the curb by "the kid." (That's what he called Vince Jr.)

"I don't want them to forget me," he'd say.

"Don't worry, you're part of the family," I'd reply.

I made sure that if he wanted to come on a tour, we always had a place for him. He was a true friend, and I appreciated what he did for me when I first came to New York.

As usual, Louie followed me into a new adventure. He never tried to involve himself in how I was used by a promoter or anything like that. He was just never into it. Some of the wrestlers or promoters were as much his friend as mine, but he had a rule: he never discussed the business. His line was always the same: "I didn't see your match." That way he'd never have to comment.

This might have been part of the reason that Louie was so popular among my peers. One time, André wanted to throw a big party in his home in the Carolinas. He invited Vince Sr., Eddie Graham, and Jim Barnett — all the big shots in the business were invited. I was also invited to attend, but I could not understand why. I still can't figure it out, except André wanted me to be there with Louie. I was the only wrestler present besides the Giant. I wish I could have thanked him for being such a good friend to me and Louie.

Louie was not only popular with the wrestlers. Before heading home from André's party, Vince Sr. asked us what we were planning to do, so we told them we were going to drive straight back to New York. Out of the blue, Vince's wife invited us to spend the night at their beach house in Maryland. Later Vince Sr. came and said to me, "I don't know what's going on. We never have wrestlers at the house. *Never.* Don't get me wrong, I'm glad you guys are coming, I'm just surprised she invited you."

We went to their house, which was beautiful, and then headed out for dinner. Louie and Juanita talked while Vince and I discussed business. She loved to read, and she got Louie going about books. They could both talk a mile a minute. We had a wonderful evening. Before going to bed, Louie said that he was looking forward to her cooking us all a nice breakfast. She answered that she didn't cook anything for anybody. Louie started in on her, joking in his way: "Well then, you're not a really good hostess . . ."

I didn't pay much attention to their conversation, and me and Vince were having a nightcap. Anyway, wouldn't you know it, the next morning Mrs. McMahon was cooking breakfast for us. Isn't that something?

I think we were different from a lot of people in the business; I wasn't obsessed with wrestling, and Louie was a real gentleman who could talk for hours about anything and everything. It must have turned the image she had of wrestlers on its head. Vince Sr. also loved Louie just as much as anyone who ever met him.

The best story of them all, for me, happened a few months later when we were visiting Florida. Vince Sr. found out we were there and he invited us, as well as my manager, the Grand Wizard Ernie Roth, to join him on his boat. Vince had an incredible house by the canal and there he was, the biggest wrestling promoter in the country, out on the ocean with his three gay friends. That blew my mind. The 1980s were just around the corner and being gay was still not easy. All four of us went out to dinner after that. It's amazing, and it's the truth.

We would just enjoy ourselves and hardly talked about wrestling when we did something like go sailing together. I think Vince appreciated that I could talk about something besides business. Louie was good for me in that regard — he always kept me grounded in reality outside the wrestling world.

As I mentioned, when I came to New York in 1979, they wanted me to wrestle the champion, Bob Backlund. I challenged him for the title a record four times in a row at Madison Square Garden. It had never been done before and has never been done since. Back then, if you didn't draw at the Garden, you wouldn't stay in a main-event program no matter what the original storyline plan might have been.

Hard to believe I was ever that young and handsome.
Singing is something that came back into my life and has filled a void.

Little drummer boy . . . I don't know if that could have worked in wrestling, but back then I would do anything to perform for an audience.

First communion was a big thing in my native Québec. I liked church and was even an altar boy.

My first job at a wrestling show: hot dog vendor.
Fortunately, I was a much better wrestler than vendor.

Killer Kowalski was my hero. He later
became my partner and, more importantly,
my friend.

Mad Dog Vachon visiting my mother around
Christmas time. Maurice was the man who
got me my big break in wrestling.

My brothers Richard, Normand, me, André, and Michel. My sisters Lise,
Claudette, Mom Simone, Dad Gérard, Annette, and Suzanne.

"Nature Boy" Buddy Rogers left quite the impression on my younger
self. It was quite humbling to work with him later on.

Traveling the world was a benefit of my job. Visiting Japan was great, though I could not have lived there as some of my contemporaries did.

*Me with the love of my life, Louie, looking great,
even if that look would not fly today.*

*About to golf with Louie and my good friend Nick Bockwinkel, who was
instrumental in making sure we had a great reputation in the business.*

*André the Giant having fun
with Louie for his birthday. As usual,
I'm laughing and having a good time.*

The Alley Fight against Sgt. Slaughter in 1981 might be the match I will be most remembered for. Photo courtesy of *Pro Wrestling Illustrated*.

Ray Stevens was the best partner a wrestler could have. He was also the best friend one could have to share all these great adventures in this crazy world. Photo courtesy of *Pro Wrestling Illustrated*.

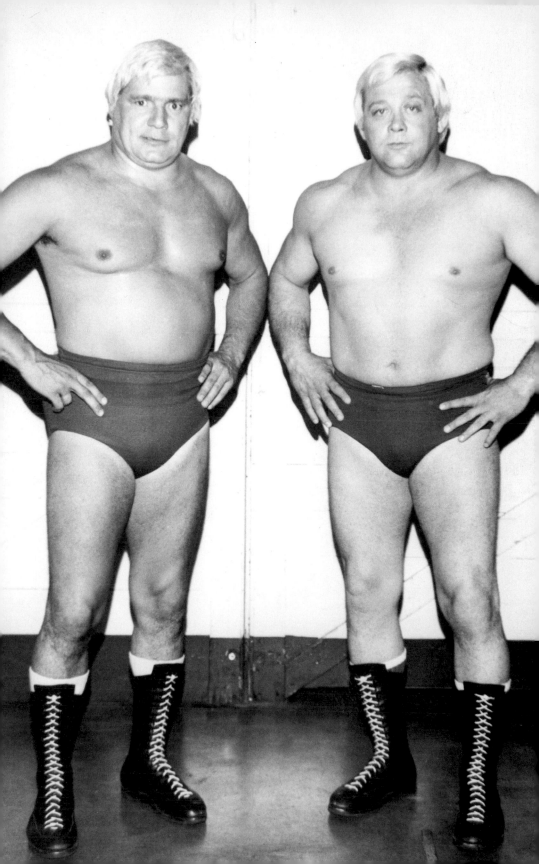

I had more than one hold in my arsenal. For a while I used the Figure Four Leg-Lock.

Photo courtesy of *Pro Wrestling Illustrated*.

Back in San Francisco for WrestleMania *in 2015, I could not
have been more emotional. In some ways, my heart will always be there.*

*Coaching Kevin Owens and other current WWE Superstars
is something I'm grateful for because I can do for them what others did
for me when I was coming up.*

*Having a blast one last time with my mentor
Maurice "Mad Dog" Vachon at the WWE Hall of Fame in 2010.*

When I came back to Montreal in the 1980s, I became "le Rêve du Québec,"
or the Dream of Québec. *People still hate that character today.*
Photo courtesy of Linda Boucher.

*I can't believe at my age
I still need to do photo shoots
for wrestling. I have been doing
this for over 58 years!*

*Working with the
NXT talent is what I enjoy
doing the most today. I see the
same dream in their eyes as
I had back in the day.*

Through the years it was with great pride I stood by Vince McMahon's side.

Humble beginnings doing commentary with Vince. No one could have guessed we would be flying in a private jet one day . . . except for Vince.

Today Vince and I still share a laugh together when we are working.

*For a long time, it was my job to make sure
that Hulk Hogan knew we had his back
as a company, and he brought this business
more notoriety than anyone else.*

I sometimes can't believe The Rock is the same person as the kid who would sit with me in the dressing room while his dad was in the ring.

Shawn Michaels and I go way back. Here we are playing around for the camera in an elevator. I'm glad that we can share laughs like this today.

Bret Hart was a special talent and we have a bond from sharing the same passion for the business. I'm glad I played a little part in him making peace with the company.

Moving was part of the deal. Louie was always ready to go even if that meant moving to the other side of the country.

Jack Lanza, Al DeRusha, Nick Bockwinkel, Bobby Heenan, Louie, me, "Cowboy" Bob Orton Jr., and Lord Alfred Hayes on the road and having fun in the AWA.

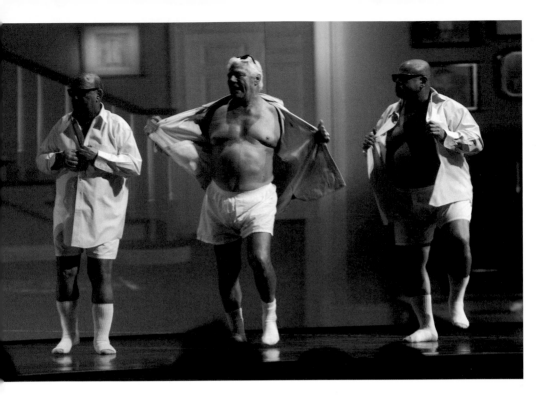

I got conned into being part of Legends' House,
*but in the end it was a great experience where I was able to finally
come out of the proverbial closet.*

*About to enjoy a great NXT show with "Nature Boy" Ric Flair
and the late great "American Dream" Dusty Rhodes.*

May 4, 2015, Pat Patterson Appreciation Night at the Bell Center in Montréal. I could not have been happier singing in front of so many people. I am always looking for the next audience to perform for.

The champion would remain in place, of course, but they would move on to the next challenger. That's how it worked. Vince Sr. liked my first match with Backlund so much we ended up having three return bouts.

The third match with Backlund along with the famous match with Slaughter I had later were my greatest moments as a wrestler. WWE has everything on tape except that third match with Backlund, and I've always been disappointed about that. In my humble opinion, we came up with one of the very best endings for a match ever. The old man — that's how I sometimes refers to Vince Sr. — wanted a third match after I had won the first match by disqualification and the second by count-out. Backlund had never lost a match at that point and he had now lost two in a row. For the third match, it was decided there would be no winner.

It was my big chance — not a lot of main-event rivalries made it to a third bout in those days.

At MSG, managers would retreat to the dressing room after the introductions, because they got so much heat from the crowd and it often led to trouble, sometimes even rioting. We got special permission for our managers to be ringside that night. The Grand Wizard would be there for me and Arnold Skaaland would be in Bob's corner. As the main-event bad guy at MSG, you exited the building hidden in an ambulance, and the driver dropped you off at your hotel. This procedure was put in place after a car was turned upside down by the crowd. On that night, we all knew that the managers' presence at ringside was like throwing a match into a powder keg, and I truly hoped it wouldn't explode.

Near the end of the match, I started to reach into my tights for the brass knuckles I'd hidden. Skaaland got on the apron to signal my cheating to the ref, and then the Grand Wizard jumped up as well. Of course, that distracted the referee who was busy telling both

*The Grand Wizard was my manager
and I was the first ever Intercontinental Champion.*

men to get down from the ring. I hit Backlund with the knucks and knocked him out cold. I went to nail Skaaland next, but he ducked and hit me with the championship he carried for Bob. So there we were, both the babyface champion and the heel contender side by side in the middle of the ring, out cold. The ref began counting us out, very slowly, hoping one of us would get to our feet before a count of ten.

By the time he got to six, the building was shaking. I was sure the roof was gonna come off — the fans wanted Backlund to start moving that bad. Everyone went on an emotional roller-coaster ride and the crowd was almost as tired as we were when the referee finally counted both of us out. After that, we had to have a final and fourth match, and I finally lost in a cage. But now that I think back, Bob Backlund never pinned me for a count of one-two-three . . . Isn't that something?

In the middle of this series with Backlund, I was actually crowned the first ever Intercontinental Champion — this also meant I was the first Intercontinental Champion to challenge the World Champion. That reminds me: the Intercontinental Championship . . . I won it in Rio de Janeiro. Which surprises me, because for some reason I don't remember ever going there. But since I am indeed the first Intercontinental Champion, and the internet says I won a tournament in Rio to be crowned the first champion, I must have been there for at least one night, right? It must have been one hell of a party with Arnold Skaaland and André the Giant if I don't remember *any* of it.

After all of these trials and tribulations, Vince Sr. finally offered me the position of color commentator for televised matches and had me doing interviews ringside.

On TV, as a rib, they had me say "Rio de Janeiro" as much as possible because I never could say it quite right. Sometimes they would tease me even more and make me do a five-minute interview with a wrestler who only spoke Spanish . . . Vince Sr. would shake his head and tell me it was no good.

"Yeah, but *you* had me do it."

So, I had become an announcer and I was now even a good guy. The Wizard had sold my contract to Lou Albano and we had a falling-out. It made my return to the Garden a big deal. I was already working as an agent at that point, because they wanted to keep me around without having me wrestling every week. They knew I could tell our audience the stories we needed to tell on television. And they didn't even care about my accent, because Bruno was *worse* than me. And before Bruno, it was Antonino Rocca, so I was *really* an improvement. OK, we were all *shit* . . .

Let me tell you, when WWE inducted Bruno Sammartino into the Hall of Fame in 2013, I was very happy. Reconnecting with him had been a long time coming, and it was fun to sit together for two hours, reminiscing. We were both happy that all the bullshit of the past was finally behind us. Whenever we see each other now, we have a blast — I tell him all my old jokes and we laugh our asses off. When I was working with Backlund in 1979, Bruno was still hot in Boston and he requested that I work with him there, instead of Backlund. He ended up losing by count-out against me — and Bruno would never lose. I truly appreciated him doing that, and I still remember it as if it was yesterday.

Perhaps the most famous match I had in WWE, however, was against Sgt. Slaughter. When it happened, I was a full-time commentator and he was doing his $5,000 Cobra Clutch Challenge. The story of his challenge went like this: he would invite a wrestler into the ring and promise that if he could escape his sleeper hold, he'd earn the five grand. Of course, no one could break the hold. Sarge was managed by my former manager, the Grand Wizard, and he was the biggest

When Vince and I started to work together it was not always easy.

bully in the business. Anyway, I was doing an interview with both of them after an opponent had just fled in fear. One thing led to another and then Slaughter slapped me, calling me "yellow." (I had refused the challenge for weeks because I considered myself retired — even though Sarge was offering me $10,000, twice as much as a regular challenger. I figured I had nothing to prove.) Naturally, I got mad at being disrespected like that, so I challenged him to go right then and there. I took off my jacket, shirt, and tie, and I let him put the Cobra Clutch on me — and the crowd whipped itself into a frenzy. I fought like crazy, with maneuvers people had never seen, to get out of that sleeper. Knowing I was finally about to break his dreaded hold, he released it and then proceeded to hit me with a chair. People were freaking out. He picked up my bloodied body and put on the Cobra Clutch once again. I went completely out. He refused to release the hold even when others climbed into the ring to try to make him stop. It was quite an eventful evening and the WWE Universe clamored for revenge. (By the way, technically, Sarge never paid me for breaking the hold. With interest, I think I'm owed quite a bit of money today.)

We had the inevitable confrontation after that on April 6, 1981, at the Garden and then we toured our rivalry around the territory . . . No rulebook could keep us in check and we were both disqualified.

Our big night at MSG came on May 4, 1981. It was booked as an Alley Fight, and there was no referee in the ring with us. I won after repeatedly hitting a bloodied Slaughter with my cowboy boot, and the Wizard finally threw in the towel on Slaughter's behalf. We won a bunch of awards that year for best match, and it also captured the imagination of the WWE universe for years to come. There is not a lot about the matches of that era that I remember, but these few are really special to me. Stories about what happened outside of the arenas — well, that's what I look back on most fondly. There's plenty of them, and they all still make me laugh.

I hurt my knee while working in New York, doing the same back-flip over the turnbuckle I'd done a thousand times before. I needed surgery — I was getting older and my body was letting me know it. Luckily, I didn't miss a lot of time, only about two weeks, because the procedure was arthroscopic.

Anyway, two days after I left the hospital, I got a call.

"Hello, sir, it's Dr. Lewis."

I could not remember if this was the doctor who had operated on me, because I had seen two. He said he had worked on my leg.

"I have to tell you something; we need you to come back to the hospital."

"Why?"

"You see, sir, we left something in your knee during the surgery. It will take only twenty minutes and everything will be fine."

I was really pissed.

"How could this happen, doc? What time should I be there tomorrow?"

"About ten should be fine."

"But I can't believe you screwed up like this, doc . . ."

The doctor burst out laughing — it was actually a friend of mine pulling a joke on me. I was relieved. If he hadn't blown his cover, I would have gone to the hospital the next day for sure. "Dr. Lewis" was, in fact, WWE Hall of Famer Arnold Skaaland. That didn't happen to me too often; I usually was the one pulling the pranks.

We were working a show in Portland, Maine, on a Sunday afternoon. Most of us were going straight back to Boston, I was driving the van and André was in the back near the big sliding door. I told him there was another car with some wrestlers just in front of us and when we passed them, we'd moon them. André was always in for a good laugh.

"OK, boss."

So he opened the door, turned his ass toward the outside, unzipped his pants, and asked me to let him know when we were ready.

As André exposed his giant ass for the whole world to see, I blew the car's horn. But, of course, it wasn't a car full of wrestlers. It was an elderly couple in the wrong place at the wrong time. He was fucking mad. I'm still laughing about this one. Sorry, André.

Rene Goulet was a funny guy and a fellow Quebecer. He was another Mad Dog protégé and worked with me as a producer for WWE. We had a show in Hartford once, on another Sunday afternoon, and it was still day when we got on the highway to head back home to Stamford. We hit some major traffic and we weren't moving.

That's when Goulet said, "*J'ai envie de caca.*" For those of you who don't speak French, that means that my friend needed to go . . . now. But there was nowhere for him to go. Poor Rene. "I have to go now; I can't hold it anymore. I'm going to do it in my pants."

I told him to take a deep breath and be patient; we were nearing an exit. He kept telling me that he wasn't going to be able to wait that long. At some point, he grabbed some Kleenex I had in the car and ordered me to stop the car right there. I pulled over on the side of the road and he jumped out, dropped his pants, and let nature take its course. Well by now, I hope you've figured out what my next move was going to be. Yes, of course, I drove off and left him all by his lonesome with his pants around his ankles. Everybody was honking their horns at him. When he was done he began to run after me, faster than a speeding bullet. I think he was even madder than André. But I would never have forgiven myself if I had missed that opportunity.

At one point, Verne Gagne began running opposition to Roy Shire. Verne was putting shows on in Oakland, and Roy had limited himself to San Francisco. Verne even took over the television in the Bay Area. I was in New York, but Verne was using Bockwinkel and Stevens in an attempt to hurt Roy and take over his cities. A week before Roy's annual battle royal, Verne announced his own battle royal in the same market. He called Vince Sr. to have me in Oakland.

I was happy with the booking — I was going to see Ray, Nick, Greg Gagne, and Bobby Heenan, while getting paid to make a trip to California. As soon as my name was advertised, Roy Shire called Vince Sr.

"You motherfucker, you let fucking Patterson work for fucking Verne Gagne! I have my own battle royal a week after. Now I've got to have Patterson as well."

Senior came to me and said, "You have to do me a big favor. You have to stay down there and work for Roy Shire in his battle royal after Verne's show. He's mad because I let you go."

I said no, I'm not doing it. I was still mad about how things ended between Roy and me.

Vince Sr. then said, "You can't do that to me. Roy's screaming. You've got to go. Please?"

Reluctantly I said yes, on the condition that I would be paid in full before I even showed up. As far as I knew, Roy was still mad at me for leaving and I didn't want him to screw with my money for revenge. I went and wrestled the battle royal in Oakland for Verne, and a week later I entered the battle royal for Roy in San Francisco. It was the last battle royal Roy ever ran.

And you won't believe who won that match.

Yes. It was me.

I wrestled for opposing promoters in the same market one week apart.

Despite all of that shit we went through together, Roy and I, he was a smart man. Maybe he was still mad at me, but he gave the fans what they wanted to see.

Even my father had accepted who I was. Still, we had never discussed the issue between us since I'd left for Boston all those years ago. Now that I was living in New York, it meant I was just a few hours away from him again. For a good part of my life, I had been under the impression that my dad loved my brother Normand and that was it. But early in my run in New York, Louie and I had my dad over. I flew him to New Jersey and took him to Madison Square Garden. And then I arranged to sit and talk with him, one-on-one. It wasn't an argument — I just calmly let him know how I felt when

I was young. I just let it all out, in a nice way. We both cried and we held hands and hugged. And then I reached into my pocket and I gave him a nice little diamond ring. And oh my God, he cried like a baby. I had never seen my father cry . . . Damn, it felt good to let that burden go.

When I lost him on March 4, 1981, it didn't register the way it did when I lost my mother. I saw him in the hospital, and then the family left to get something to eat and when we came back, he was gone. At the end, he was still the same: a very stern man. He was hard-headed and he always would be. I wish he were here to read this today. We ran out of the time we needed to get close, but at least we had closure.

On the business front, I was wrestling less and less. My friend Gorilla Monsoon was in charge of television and Lord Alfred Hayes worked as a commentator, so I kept working behind the scenes with my friends. On top of my duties as a commentator, Vince Sr. asked me to go on the road full-time as a producer. He needed someone to be in charge of the show, someone he could trust. I enjoyed that very much, and when George Scott quit, I moved up to working in the office . . . But that's a story for later.

I think I had my last matches (until the Attitude Era and the stooges stuff I did with Gerald Brisco) around 1987, when I worked some of the WWE shows in Montréal. On August 31, 1987, I had a match against Brutus Beefcake with Mr. T as the referee at the Montréal Forum. It seemed like a fitting end to my active career, wrestling in the city where my dream had started almost thirty years before. And Mr. T was a big star. Not too bad for a local boy like me. (I lost some hair in that one, though.) The attendance was 14,624. Not bad either.

I wrestled all the top wrestlers in our business, so I must have been good, right? Being gay never had anything to do with it. It

*Vince and I started from very different backgrounds,
but we became a great team and, more importantly, great friends.*

just meant I had to work harder and laugh in the face of abuse. I'm proud of the fact that I always left a territory of my own accord: I was never given notice.

That young kid from Montréal who loved wrestling had been in the main event at Madison Square Garden in New York City, and that still means something to me. When the old man thanked me and told me how good my matches with Backlund and Slaughter were, in my mind I knew everything had been worth it.

Sure enough, the wrestling business was not done with me. I was about to start the second part of my career, the one that is apparently never going to end. But before I get into that, I have a few more stories I want to share with you about my travels.

AROUND THE WORLD
...AND BACK!

"I've lived a life that's full"

What a way to make a living, doing what you love, while traveling all over the world, meeting people and making friends while staying in some of the most incredible hotels on the planet. There is no way I could have envisioned that when I left Montréal or even when I was lying on my bed looking up at the ceiling in my little apartment in Boston. I've always hated routine and I'm always up for something new, so traveling was usually fun for me.

But, strangely, tours of Japan were difficult for me. They were just too intense, too much about wrestling. You stay with wrestlers, you wrestle, you travel to a wrestling show by train, you wrestle, you take a bus to another wrestling show, where there's . . . even more wrestling. I can't live and talk about the business twenty-four-seven; I need a break. That was the hardest part for me. The language barrier didn't help either. In 1968, for my first tour, it was a big culture shock. In Japan, there are regular hotels just like we have, and there are also Japanese hotels. In those, you sleep on the floor with a rice pillow and a tatami for a mattress. The toilet is standing only — there's no time to read, let me tell you. The food was also a challenge for me. There's a lot of fish and I didn't like fish when I first went. I'm glad I've experienced it, but it wasn't for me. I could not have worked in Japan full-time like others did.

I also found it hard to work in front of a crowd that barely reacted and just quietly enjoyed the spectacle. I was always more of a storyteller, and my matches were never about how flashy I could be, so it was hard for me to get a reaction.

Yet I still managed to have fun with my friends. André knew exactly where every bar in the country was located. Me, I would rather just drink at the hotel bar and not bother going out. But one night he told me, "Boss, we're going out tonight." You didn't say no when André said something like that.

He took me to every godforsaken bar in Tokyo. They were all very small places and everywhere we went, everyone knew him. We got a good table right away — they knew what he needed to be comfortable. We had fun, but when it was about 4 a.m., I pleaded with André to head back to the hotel. I needed to sleep.

"No. I have to bring you to one more place, boss."

"OK, André, you're the boss."

André was always *the* boss, even though he called everyone else boss.

We took a taxi. André was all contorted to fit in the small vehicle. Seeing him trying to keep his big frame inside was hilarious, and that alone made the trip priceless. It took us quite some time to get there, and I was becoming very impatient.

"Don't worry, boss, we'll be there soon. It will be worth it."

We stopped in front of an office building, a big skyscraper with big glass doors and everything. I said, "What the hell? Where are we going, a doctor's office? Doesn't look like they have a bar in there."

"Don't worry, boss, don't worry."

We went to the fifth floor, then walked down what seemed like the longest corridor ever. Finally André knocked on the last door. The door swung open and there it was: a small bar with a drag queen show hiding inside that impressive, conservative building. André loved the place because no one would ever bother him, and he could drink in peace. He was sure I would love it too and he was right. They took care of him like royalty, giving him more attention than had been shown to us in all the other bars.

My friend Ricky Hunter was booked in Japan because I put in a good word for him. On that tour, we were staying in a Japanese-style hotel. During dinner, he dropped his keys and I picked them up without him noticing. As he continued to drink, I went to his room and I made it look like someone had robbed him. I went back to

Traveling with André in Japan was always interesting.

the bar and sometime later we both went upstairs to bed. I had the room beside his and as we were saying good night, he realized that he couldn't find his key. He went downstairs to get another and I pretended to go to bed. Obviously, I was in my room and waiting, because I knew I was about to have a front-row seat for the upcoming spectacle. As expected, he banged on my door, yelling that his room had been robbed. I played it cool and didn't laugh, even suggesting guys who he had a little bit of heat with on the tour as possible culprits. (I liked to stir a little shit in my day.)

Later, we laughed a lot; at least I did.

While in Australia and Japan, I got to know and team with my idol, Killer Kowalski. We didn't have much in common: he didn't drink and he was a vegetarian. Still, I had found ways to have fun with him even though he was a serious man. In Australia, all the wrestlers went to a very nice family restaurant and he went too. The staff knew exactly what he wanted because he had spent quite some time explaining that they needed to take the meat out of all their recipes for him. You know me well enough by now, right? You guessed it: if he got up to go to the bathroom, I would make sure the waiter added chicken to his meal. Killer would then get hot, because they had messed up his order. One time, he got so hot, he even went to the kitchen to complain to the chef.

San Francisco and Montréal are my favorite cities in North America, and Sydney, Australia, is my favorite city in the rest of the world. Australia was an easy place to live compared to Japan, and on top of it, the fans really enjoyed our show.

I went three times — in 1966, 1967, and 1968 — while the territory was still very popular. Jim Barnett was in charge and he had a strong relationship with Roy Shire in San Francisco. Australia was quite the experience. I was with Kowalski and Gorilla Monsoon. If I went to a bar and spent twenty dollars, I could buy a round for the whole place. It's easy to have fun and make friends like that. Those long tours were not easy on my relationship with Louie, but he knew it was part of the deal. I would always come back to him, he knew, but I'm sure it was hard to be alone while I was on the other side of the world.

Each time I went overseas, it was for a six-week tour. I met people and had fun in every city, every night. Australia was very open-minded for the time. I always found a gay bar, though some cities had more than others. Australia is a big country and we almost never drove and had to fly everywhere. It was the first time I worked for Jim Barnett, but our paths crossed again in Florida and New York. I loved my time there and it gave me the chance to do some of my first trips just for fun. When I was in school, we had been collecting funds for the poor people of Tahiti. For some reason, that remained stuck in my head for a long time. The last time I went to Australia, I met two lesbian strippers who happened to be from Tahiti. I know it seems unbelievable, but that's the kind of thing that happened to me. Usually, when you're done working a tour, you just want to go straight home. But they offered to have me visit Tahiti before I went back to the States and to let me stay with them at their place. To my own surprise, I said yes. My two-day stay turned into a full week. I just loved it. Everyone spoke French; we went to the nudist beach every day; and everyone was friendly. I didn't get to do a lot of personal traveling like that during my career, but I appreciated the opportunity when it came up.

Gorilla Monsoon was a great guy — that can't be said often enough. We became good friends. He found those Australian tours very hard. He was a big man and over there it's hot all the time — and he was not into going out as he was totally faithful to his wife. At the time, he had a big boil under his butt cheek and he was really suffering. Because of his size, he had trouble putting ointment on it and bandaging it. When he told me about the pain he was in, and how difficult it was for him to get this thing to heal, I said, "I will do that for you."

"I can't ask you that," he said.

"You are a friend; it's nothing; don't worry about it."

He truly missed his family on those long trips. They were wonderful, and Louie and I went to their place for dinners often. We were very close with all of them, and I still miss him very much.

In Australia, wrestling was a respected business, and there was a lot of very public travel. Because of that, Barnett had established a very strict dress code for his workers. I was never against the dress code Barnett demanded of us. In fact, I loved getting nice suits made while I was working over there. Wrestling was big business, and we needed to look like professionals. In a typical week, we would fly from Sydney to Melbourne for a big show, then fly to Perth, Adelaide, Brisbane, and back to Sydney. We would often do six shows, and two different sets of television, in between all that traveling. I respected Barnett: he thought the world of me, and I wanted to look the part of the star. The wrestling business is all about image, and I think it's only prudent to think about that when you are a promoter.

Roy Shire's television shows aired in the Samoan Islands, and Peter Maivia was such a star there that we ended up setting up a tour in his home country. We landed at 2 a.m. at a very small airport and there were 2,000 people waiting for us, sitting on the roof. Everywhere Peter went, people were screaming. On a tour the following day, thousands of people followed us around hoping to catch a glimpse of him. It was amazing.

I spent the week with Maivia and we were treated like kings. We had one match together, and I was his partner, thank God. I would not have wanted to be his opponent during the tour for all the money in the world. Our opponents were in danger the whole time we were on the island. We had to hide them to make sure nothing bad happened; the bad guys would actually have rocks thrown at them during the show if the fans got mad enough. This was very scary for everyone; even us good guys could get hit. And remember, some Samoans kill wild pigs by throwing rocks at them and they learn that skill at a very young age . . . The danger was very real.

I stayed at the home of one of Peter's close friends and my every need was attended to, like I were some kind of god or something. I remember my host asking if I ever had vodka and coconut juice. I said no, but told him that I loved vodka. (In fact, it's still my favorite drink.) Now he had to make me one. So one of his kids climbed thirty feet up a tree just to get us a fresh coconut, right there in front of me. They chopped the top off, filled it up with ice and added some vodka and let it soak a little. Let me tell, you can't stop at just one — it was as good as I was told.

Many of the houses on Samoa back then didn't have walls, just straw roofs. When you were born and raised in Montréal in the forties and fifties, it was quite something to visit a place like that.

We played many jokes on the plane back to Australia to pass the time. A fellow Quebecer, Brute Bernard, who was completely bald, made the mistake of falling asleep. I drew a bunch of veins on his head and then covered his head with his hat. When we got to Australia, he asked me to look out for his luggage while he went to the restroom. A few moments later, the whole airport heard the big scream from the bathroom. Everyone laughed.

In 1981, WWE sent wrestlers to the Universal Wrestling Association in Mexico. I was still a versatile wrestler and a former

Intercontinental Champion, so I ended up working in Mexico a few times. I really didn't like it. The style there was so different — lots of flashy moves — and that's not what I was good at. I wrestled El Canek, one of the biggest stars in the country, for the UWA Championship at Palacio de los Deportes. We had a good match and drew 18,000 fans. I also teamed with Bob Backlund against Canek and Perro Aguayo in Arena Mexico, the Mexican equivalent of working the main event at Madison Square Garden against the likes of Randy Savage and the Ultimate Warrior. I was able to enjoy my stay, since we had a nice hotel and the weather was great, but it really wasn't for me.

Being based in New York also gave me an opportunity to work in Montréal after I had not been home in a long time, especially not to wrestle. Frank Valois and Gino Brito had taken over the territory, and André the Giant was in business with them. Vince Sr. asked me if I wanted to go to Montréal, suggesting that I could make sure André's best interests were being taken care of while having some fun. "Just go there, wrestle, and have a good time," he said.

I knew I wanted a break from being a commentator, and since my in-ring career was pretty much done in New York, it was the perfect opportunity. Everything was great — just seeing a typical Québec snack bar and its steamed hot dogs made me feel fantastic. And to eat them again . . . They were just as good as I remembered from my childhood, heading back to my family in the cold after watching wrestling at the Forum. I was home.

For the first time in my life, I truly discovered the province of Québec, going to Granby, Sherbrooke, Rimouski, Trois-Rivières, Québec City, and many other towns. After teaming with Raymond Rougeau for a while, we became opponents.

I became *le Rêve du Québec* or the Dream of Québec if you will. I had fun with that. People still talk to me about it today when I'm home, or when I meet another Quebecer on the road, or in Florida where I spend half of the year. It was more than thirty years ago and people still remember how passionately they hated me back then. I must have been doing something right . . . Of course, I came up with the idea because of Dusty Rhodes, the American Dream. But Pat Patterson being Rêve du Québec was the opposite of Dusty's gimmick, since I had an English name while speaking French. It was the perfect bad-guy image for me. Since I was in Montréal for the entire summer, Louie came up and helped me rediscover my roots.

One night in Rimouski, I came up with the idea of doing a boxing match with Raymond Rougeau and we decided to make it a ten-round decision.

After three rounds, I couldn't take it anymore. I didn't know Raymond had a real boxing training. I could not touch him and he would sting me right in the face every now and then with a smirk. Anyway, I said fuck that and just stayed down for the count. All the other wrestlers were watching from the back and everyone was having a good laugh at my expense.

I respected Raymond a lot after that. When Vince Jr. asked about talent from Québec, he was at the top of my list. If WWE wanted to draw in Montréal, we needed local stars, so that's why we got the Rougeau brothers, Dino Bravo, and Rick Martel. It was never about getting my friends to New York, as some said or thought. We had a business to run and WWE was successful running the Montréal Forum monthly for years because we did what needed to be done.

Another benefit of working in Montréal that summer was that my good friend Lord Alfred Hayes was also there. We roomed together in Rimouski one night. I don't remember much about what happened, but when I woke up the next morning, the television was on and Alfred was not in his bed. Neither was his mattress or the sheets and pillows for that matter. I wondered if he was OK, or if he'd been kidnapped or something.

I went into the bathroom, and there he was, sleeping on his mattress on the floor. Apparently, I had been snoring so loudly that after trying to wake me and turning the television on to mask the sound coming out of me, he just gave up and barricaded himself in the restroom. Apparently I can play pranks in my sleep.

Alfred had a fantastic brand-new van for our travels around *la belle province*. In the back, we played cards and drank beer. There was a hidden compartment under the ashtray. I started stuffing all kinds of garbage in there, especially empty beer bottles. After a few days, Alfred looked at me and said, "Patrick, I don't understand; there's a weird noise and this van is brand-new. It's like glass clicking together." I began laughing so hard he knew — I had to tell him what the noise was.

Lord Alfred never swore, which made him a funny companion for me. Not that I ever treated him differently from my other friends . . . I gave him plenty of opportunity to curse me, but he never did.

Today I like to go on cruises every chance I get. Recently I stopped in Spain and wanted to take a day trip to Fatima in Portugal to see the shrine there. I called a taxi and only one driver spoke English. "It's a two- or three-hour drive," he said. "It's the anniversary. There will be thousands and thousands of people. I can take you where St. Jacques [James the Apostle] is buried in the mountains, if you like, instead?" I said yes.

People would usually walk 1,000 miles up to that church in Santiago. We found a little restaurant there. This is where *coquilles St-Jacques*, or scallops in English, became famous. So the driver and I ate, drank wine, and had fun. When we got back, we were singing together like two old friends, I gave him a $100 tip. It was worth every penny.

Traveling the world blindly and boldly, making new friends and having fun without any worries, is how I try to live my life. I still travel a lot for work, and I particularly enjoy the European tours. In 2014, I was in Belgium and doing the ring announcing in English for the Intercontinental Championship. Then I hit my forehead and said I was sorry in French, "*Je m'excuse.*" I got the biggest reaction. People were so happy to hear someone from WWE speaking French. It was a special and unique moment for them and for me. I went on and made a small speech in French.

But we only did that once — I'm getting too old for that shit . . .

WHAT DOES A VICE
PRESIDENT DO, ANYWAY?

"And more, much more than this, I did it my way"

I had great experiences almost everywhere I worked because I felt wanted. But being in New York with Vince McMahon Sr. was very special. If you can make it there you can make it anywhere, as the song says, and to this day, it does mean something in our business to become somebody in New York.

People around me kind of knew I was gay, but I never told anyone in confidence I was. Until appearing on *Legends' House* on the WWE Network, I had never said those words out loud for everyone to hear — but that's a story for later. When I started to work behind the scenes for Vince Sr., I decided to tell him everything, and he simply said, "I already know. Now get back to work." He never asked any questions, and he clearly couldn't care less that I was gay. We had fun and worked well together. I was loyal and I did my job.

We used to tape our television programs on back-to-back days in Allentown and Bethlehem, Pennsylvania. In between those days, we stayed at a hotel in Reading, Pennsylvania. We used to go to a restaurant that stayed open just for us after the first show. Vince Sr. would invite a small circle of people, maybe eight or ten guys each time. The point was just to have a good time telling stories, drinking, and eating gargantuan meals. The gathering kept the place open until at least until 2 a.m. I was finally invited, but, as far as I knew, Louie was not. Arnold Skaaland was in charge of these little get-togethers, and as he was leaving the taping, he told me he would see me at the restaurant. I politely said I would not be coming, since I could not just drop Louie at the hotel and go by myself.

"Hell no, you're coming. Louie is coming with me right now to set things up."

From that point on, Skaaland and Louie became close friends.

Television taping day was a long haul, and the word started to get around that Louie was a barber. Like everywhere else we went, Louie was friendly with everybody. One day, as I was walking by the dressing room I discovered Louie cutting hair. There was a lineup of wrestlers, waiting their turn.

"What's going on here?" I asked.

"They've been bugging me for so long, I decided I should just do it," Louie said.

After that, Louie always set up a makeshift barbershop backstage at every taping, so the wrestlers could look their best.

We became a trustworthy part of the team, and we did it without kissing anyone's ass.

As Vince Jr. began taking over for his dad, I was already an established presence backstage, in the role of what we called an agent back then and a producer today.

A few weeks before Vince Sr. passed away, we were working like crazy getting the national expansion under way with big television tapings all over the country. The old man called me from his deathbed. He wanted to make sure I would do something for him.

"Pat, make sure they take good care of André. André is our man, you know. I know Junior wants to do too much sometimes, so please keep an eye on my son, too."

"Don't worry, sir, I will always be there for them."

I get all choked up when I think about this, and it shows you how deep my relationship runs with that family. Until the day I die, I have that promise to live up to. On May 4, 2015, on Pat Patterson Appreciation Night, Vince Jr. said I was a member of his family. I feel exactly the same way, but it was very special for me to have him express it like that, in front of fans in my hometown of Montréal. He also mentioned Louie on that night and that touched me deeply. I can finally be proud of who Louie and I were.

When Vince Sr. first put me on commentary with Jr., I didn't know him very well. He can seem kind of distant when you don't know him, and I didn't know how we would click. Apparently we did.

At first, when he took over, some of the talent was going nuts. *The kid is going to kill the business . . . The kid doesn't know what he's doing . . .* I heard it more than a few times.

Everyone was knocking him, but he did it *his* way, and he *was* right in the end. When we started taping television in St. Louis, many of the other promoters in the different territories across the country got nervous. They were very unhappy, but he stuck to his vision. The idea that he was making the old guard unhappy never undermined his determination. All of those guys would have done the same if they had had his vision and his dedication.

I made my home in Florida at the time, and on the road I worked as an agent with Jay Strongbow, Rene Goulet, and Jack Lanza. In 1985, George Scott was Vince's first right-hand man in the office, but that didn't last. The first time I went north to help Vince after Scott left, Vince was far behind, trying to do everything by himself.

I had ten days off from the road and I told him that if he wanted, I would use that time off to help him in the office in Stamford. I explained that I thought I could help him with production, in the hope that he could take a breather and catch up on the rest of his workload. No one else ever offered to work on their days off and, let me tell you, I didn't have to offer twice.

I went to work in the basement because I could smoke there. (Vince hates smoking. I always find a place to hide to get a quick smoke, even today. When we are in his limo, Vince complains about my breath, even when I chew gum trying to hide it. He must have a bionic nose or something. "I still smell the cigarette, damn it.") I did my thing: I started to map out the next two months of shows. Vince would come down and sit with me while I worked. He never once complained about my smoking, and he watched and he learned. He was impressed by my vision. Some have said that if someone has a single idea, I might turn it into a story that will go on for the next six months. Now I don't know about that, and I sure don't agree with everything that was ever said about me, but in this case I will agree and say that I am a very creative person.

After those ten days in the basement, Vince told me I was not going back out on the road.

"What do you mean?"

"You're working in the office now."

My heart almost fell out of my chest. All my life, I tried to escape white-collar jobs, and I still end up in an office? Isn't life something? I am a team player and this was where I was needed the most, so I agreed to the change.

I moved into a Connecticut apartment with Louie. We didn't sell our home in Florida right away; I didn't know if an office job was going to work out for me. But it did and we sold the house and bought a condominium close to the WWE office we used to call Titan Tower. I hated living in Stamford — I'm just a regular guy, and everyone has big money there. I never quite felt comfortable in that kind of crowd.

After three weeks working in the office, Vince and his wife, Linda, took me out for dinner. She was the one who told me.

"Pat, we have something important to tell you. As of now, you are a senior vice president for the company."

"Vince . . . Linda . . . I have no idea what this means."

"Linda, didn't I tell you it wouldn't mean anything to him?" Vince said. We all had a good laugh. And then he started to explain to me what a vice president was. "It's a great title. It means we have confidence in you and that you are an important part of the company."

"Vince, I just know wrestling . . . I'm not sure I can be a good senior vice president."

Apparently, I was wrong.

In the office, I took care of everything regarding the talent side of the business since I knew what it was like for the boys out on the road. I knew a few ways we could immediately make things better and get them to the next city on the schedule more efficiently. The timing was great: my body could not keep on wrestling forever, but my mind was still as sharp as ever. As Mad Dog Vachon used to say, "Getting old is not for sissies." I'm allowed to say that, right?

I was very fortunate to get this opportunity, and the reality is not all former wrestlers are qualified for an office job. The transition meant I could stay at the top level in a business that I love. At age fifty, there are no main-event matches anymore . . . at least not for 99.9% of us.

Working in the office was something new and interesting for me. I did a lot of my work with Vince at his house, which made it a lot more fun. There were so many meetings when we were at the office, and that got old very quickly. At least for me it did. Still, I had to meet and work with a lot of new people with many different skills, all of whom were important in the company's growth. During that time, I really had no idea how a senior vice president was supposed to act . . .

Just to show you how clueless I was, I would often have so much clerical stuff to do that I could barely keep up. Then one day Vince checked in on me and found me filing. He said, "Why are you doing all of that? That's why you have a secretary working for you." I didn't even know what I should or should not ask the secretary to do. Don't laugh, it's true — but at least I knew the important stuff about the show.

In those early days, I did everything in the office at one point or another, including the payroll. And essentially I was working on talent relations before there even was such a department. At that time, talent relations was me telling guys to do their job on the road, in every sense of the word, while attempting to get them to call me at home as little as possible. I was the point person for the producers who were on the road. Talent would call me for all sorts of nonsense, like helping them find the closest gym, even after I had clearly let them know that wasn't my responsibility. Not so glamorous, is it?

I was also the de facto company travel agent. When someone missed a plane or if the plane was delayed, I was the man. The producers would call me looking for a missing talent, and the talent would call to tell me what was going on and why they were late. I had to find solutions for everyone and get them in communication with each other. Before cell phones, communication on the road was no fun at all — especially when you were everybody's contact person. Even I have an iPhone today, and let me tell you, the kids have it easy . . .

In 1989, we were running four shows in the Northeast on New Year's Eve. To make it even more fun for me, we also had the biggest snowstorm in years. No one could get anywhere. That's also the year I had the brilliant idea to invite all of my brothers and sisters to Connecticut for the first time to celebrate the new year. I ended up spending my evening on the phone speaking with talent and coordinating with the office. Again and again, time after time, I said the words "There's nothing they can do" and "We're all stuck" and "I'll keep you posted." On another line, I kept telling Vince that we needed to cancel everything, but he wanted to wait a little longer.

After three hours with no improvement, we finally canceled three of the four shows because not enough talent could get to those venues. Vince's patience saved one show. It was a goddamn nightmare. The following day, we were able to get people going again, so they could get to the next town.

Even without a snowstorm, there were road issues to deal with on a regular basis. One time, the British Bulldogs called to say they'd lost Matilda, the pet bulldog that was their mascot.

"What the fuck? How do you lose a dog on a plane?" I asked.

"We don't know what's going on, Pat; she didn't come with the luggage. We have to wait until we hear back from the people at the airport. At best we're going to be late for the show," they said.

The airport staff eventually found the dog safe and sound, but not before my life was made miserable for a few hours. On one of the worst of these kinds of occasions — because Matilda was lost more than once — airport personnel ended up delivering the dog to the arena a few minutes before Davey Boy and Dynamite were to make their entrance for the main event. The dog almost didn't make its booking . . . And I thought I had seen everything by then.

Almost all of the talent would call me, asking about the direction of their career or what Vince had planned and more often than not, I didn't have an answer or wasn't allowed to answer. I always told the guys to ask Vince the next time they saw him. And that's part of the reason why I never wanted to have the "boss" title. At the end of the day, Vince always had the final word. When taping television, I was also dealing with all the local talent brought in as enhancement for our *Superstars*. They were all hoping to be discovered and that took a lot of time to manage as well.

When that wasn't enough, I would even get jokes played on me.

One time, Vince was having a meeting with the Moondogs, Rex and Spot. They started to run tons of crazy ideas past him. Vince didn't have the time to listen to everything they were saying and cut them off. "It's good stuff, please run it by Pat." After I got through with them, I tried to figure out what Vince liked about their suggestions. When I spoke to Vince later, I said, "You mean to tell me you liked their ideas?"

"Well . . . I just wanted you to listen to them."

He had thrown me to the Moondogs . . . It was a harmless prank, and we laughed about it. At the end of the day, that's all that mattered.

I remember another time when, thirty minutes before the show was to begin, there was no ring at the arena. The truck had gotten lost. And who do they call? Me. The show was in North Dakota, and Stu Hart was the one bringing the ring. At the office, I got word he was going to be late, but he never actually made the show. We had to put mats down on the floor. We had our Superstars do matches like it was Olympic wrestling. The fans were actually happy to see such a unique display — and that's what's important when the show is over. That kind of thing happened to me too when I was a wrestler — you might not have the type of match you'd planned, but you can do something to send the customer home happy. That kind of stuff happened more often than you'd think, but most of the time it wound up being nothing more than a close call.

One time, a number of Superstars were late for a show in Dayton, Ohio. We were actually missing half the crew. After two matches, we had an intermission, then there were two more matches. So then I had the ring crew "work" to "repair" the ring. But they were actually stalling to buy us time. It wasn't broken and nothing needed to be fixed.

There was one show in Toronto when, by the opening bell, the only Superstar in the building was The Honky Tonk Man. Everyone else had been held up at the border. I finally got the call that they were on their way, but I again had to buy some time. So I sent Honky out there and he must have stalled, and sung, and sung again, for close to thirty minutes. Every time it looked like he was done, he would come back to the ring and tell the crowd they were such a beautiful audience that they deserved an encore — and then he would sing again, one "last" time. People wanted to kill him.

When Vince Jr. campaigned to end regulation, I was cool with the decision. I knew firsthand how most of the "athletic commissions" were trying to take advantage of us and our success. But I still really don't like to publicly discuss the inner workings of our business. When I see a good magician, I don't want him to explain everything to me; it takes away from the beauty of his performance.

When we first started running nationwide, it was the local promoters who controlled those athletic commissions. The commissioners would make it extra hard for us to run their friends' territory. One time in Louisville, I was told that if the doctor wasn't showing up, they were going to pull the plug on the show.

"That's not my problem," I told him. "You hired the doctor, right? You make sure he shows up. If you want to cancel the show, you asshole, you'll be the one getting into the middle of the ring to announce it. Fans are going to jump on you, not on me."

He became defiant. "Don't try to be smart with me."

"I'm not trying to be smart; I'm just running a business."

They gave us a hard time every time we came to their city. I hated all of them because they were acting dishonestly, trying to prevent

Enjoying a drink after work with my friend Kevin Dunn on the company private plane.

our business from growing, even when we made them money. Some of the commissioners would take advantage of their position by bringing kids and family members backstage, and I would make sure they were kicked out. That was bullshit — they didn't belong in the dressing room. All they were supposed to do was license the wrestlers and then their job was done. They would threaten me with suspension and I would tell them to try; I wasn't the one in the wrong. Anyway, when the office spoke out about the entertainment part of what we do and got rid of most of the commissions, I was all for it because it made my job a lot easier not having to deal with all that pain-in-the-ass bullshit.

When Vince Jr. took over, we were taping television in small buildings. We had a few cameramen, and Kevin Dunn's father, Dennis, was in charge. That's how Kevin got into the business. He started at the bottom and worked his way up from there. Today, Kevin is executive vice president of television production. Vince started to change the camera angles and added more cameras. The intention was to change the way the product looked on TV — make it look better than ever. Everyone thought Vince was out of his mind, but he knew exactly what he was doing. All other wrestling programs had the same look from one territory to the next, with interviews always taking place near the ring in front of the people. We would record hours of interviews backstage, with all the guys tying what they said to their upcoming appearances in the different markets and then we aired each in the appropriate city. It was an unbelievable time for the company, and I believe we achieved so much with so little. It got to where we were running four towns a night almost seven days a week. We run two shows a day today — and the company has more resources than it had back then.

My duties also included putting the matches together for each show, specifically ordering each card in just the right way. And I had to communicate how the office wanted the matches to take place to the producers on the road. By that point, producers no longer had to carry the gate receipts with them; they were transferred to the company's bank account directly. When I was first running small towns for Vince Jr., the box office would give you the money in cash, $5,000 or $6,000 each time, and you would carry it with you on the road until you returned to Connecticut.

I was in San Jose one night with André and we went to one of my favorite restaurants. I had a briefcase filled with $60,000 in gate money with me. We had a good time and André picked up the tab as usual. I had the briefcase under my chair the whole night. At the end of the evening, we went our separate ways. I got back to my hotel, undressed, and got in bed. Of course, I would always hide the briefcase under my bed for the night . . .

That's when I realized that — yes, you've probably figured it out — I had left the briefcase at the restaurant. I jumped right out of bed and drove all the way there. The place was closed, but luckily there was still a cleaning crew working. I banged on the windows to get their attention but they just made signs for me to go away. I started screaming for them to come to the goddamn door. I was finally able to explain that I'd forgotten my briefcase earlier in the evening. They let me in and it was right there under the chair where I'd left it. I was so relieved.

Even though I was primarily working from the office, I was traveling so much that people always wanted me to bring them back something. There was this one guy working in the office who loved to smoke pot and play golf. Louie and this guy were friends and would play golf on a regular basis. He said to me, "You're going to a show in New Orleans, and I've got a friend who lives there. He's going to give you a couple joints for me."

"I don't smoke it, sell it, or carry it — so forget about it."

"Please, Pat, it's only a few joints."

When I go to the show in New Orleans, his friend came to see me and he handed me the biggest bag of pot I have ever seen in my life. Just a few joints, my ass.

I was pissed about being put in that situation, and then the guy just disappeared. After the event, the wrestlers went out to party on Bourbon Street. I was the last one to leave the building before joining the crew for a few drinks. I've never done drugs, but I've also never said no to a good drink after a hard day of work. Before I went out, I hid the pot under the spare tire in the trunk of the rental car. I was scared about getting pulled over, so I wanted to be able to say that it had been left in the rental by someone else if something happened. Brilliant? You have no idea . . .

The following day, I flew home. Upon taking off, I realized I had left the whole bag of pot in the trunk of the car. For a moment, it was as if time had stopped. When I got home, both Louie and his friend were waiting for me at the airport. They were happy to see me until I explained what had happened — in fact, they didn't believe me and were sure I was trying to play a joke on them. Then I got nervous. What would the rental company do if they found the pot in the car? They had my address and everything they needed to trace it to me. But I never heard about it, so I'm pretty sure somebody was pleasantly surprised. It's amazing when fiction becomes reality, but I made sure to never be in that position again.

Running that many towns each night was crazy and it put a lot of pressure on everyone. It was a pain in the ass, too, in the end. We eventually started to cut back. We were flying all those guys into each town from everywhere, and frankly we could have replaced many with local talent and saved a lot of money. So finally I asked the travel department (we had one by then) to send me a report about what we were really spending. I went to Vince with the numbers.

"Do you know how much money we spend running four towns a night?"

"Oh my God. We're going to need to cut back."

Not long after that, we made a list of people, fifteen or eighteen of them, that we had no choice but to give notice to. I had to tell all of them to get in a line outside of Vince's office. Everyone was scared. And it was difficult. But it needed to be done.

I worked a crazy schedule for a few years. I ended up quitting quite a few times, but Vince always wanted me back. If I was in Vince's shoes, I know I would have wanted a friend like me working by my side. Someone who doesn't blow smoke up your ass to get ahead. Someone who can be around me for two days and not speak a word to me because he knows I'm busy. Someone I could laugh with or talk about anything outside business. Someone who doesn't argue with me, but makes suggestions that have the best interest of the company at heart. Since he's busy all the time, I think he needs someone who can be there when he needs him to be there.

I think we did all right over the years.

Just to show you how we worked, one time I got to Vince's place at 8 a.m. to start work, and at 10 a.m. he was still on the phone in his office and hadn't acknowledged me. I got up and left. He called me that night around six.

"I'm sorry, Pat, I just finished my calls."

"And I got the hell out of there."

He told me I was right and that was it.

He's Vince, and he's the boss, but I'm not going to wait for him forever. There was no official schedule that I had to follow, but that also meant that there was an "anything goes" understanding between us.

We were at the gate in Houston once, waiting for our plane with forty-five minutes to kill. I decided to go to the restroom and smoke a cigarette. You could do that back then. Someone took the stall right beside me. That person spoke.

"Patrick . . . open up your book. We're going to check our numbers to see if we should run that town again after tonight."

"Vince, you gotta be kidding . . . ?"

We were talking business while we're both doing our business. To this day, he laughs when I tell people that story. We were close, that's for sure. A little too close for comfort sometimes. That's what happen when you're working with a workaholic — at least when you get along with him.

Another time, we were on a plane when, almost as soon as we took off, Vince fell asleep. Yes, he does sleep . . . occasionally. I jumped at the chance to hang out with the rest of the crew in the back. As I made my move, Vince stirred and said, "Where are you going?"

"Vince, go back to sleep. I'm just going to the restroom." I went to the back to order a drink. It was a rare moment to kick back and relax. I could never seem to get away to take a real break.

As you may have figured out, Vince doesn't do anything quite like anyone else. Once a month, he went to New York to get a haircut at a classic barbershop, but it was also very expensive. We left the office in a limousine to go to New York City and worked all the way there. While he was in the barbershop, I walked around and enjoyed myself. After the haircut, it was usually 6:30 or 7 p.m.

"Vince, can we get a cocktail or something?" I once asked.

To my surprise, he said yes. One drink became two and then two became four. It turned into a big party. Then it was: where could we go next to have a good meal and an even better drink? By the time we got home, we were drunk. And we'd had fun — and as a bonus for us both, the workaholic took a little time off.

Early on, I had the office right next to Vince's, the only one with a window. The only one with a window that opened so I could smoke in my office. But Vince still knew I was smoking, because the smoke passed right by his window. I ended up having to go outside to smoke like everyone else. I was probably one of the very few people whose smoking Vince tolerated.

It's no joke: he truly hates it. If I was driving us around, I occasionally needed to stop to have a cigarette — but I also needed an excuse for making the stop. If Vince had fallen asleep, he would always notice when we exited the highway. Now that I think about it, I'm not sure I can call what he does "sleeping."

"What are we doing, Patrick?"

"I'm hungry; I want to grab breakfast."

"Patrick, I think you want to smoke."

"Good idea, Vince. I will do both."

Sometimes, it would be to get coffee; other times because nature was calling — but, as we've established, that was not the best excuse because he would join me to work anyway.

Kevin Dunn was the third man on our team. If I was Vince's right-hand man, Kevin was the left. As a producer, he's responsible for every last thing that goes on television. *Everything.* Consider the number of hours of programming we've done over the years: the level of responsibility he's had on his shoulders is mind-boggling. When you're in charge of everything, it is impossible to make everyone happy. They had to let go of a few people not too long ago — I was surprised and asked Kevin why. He simply said that he was doing his job. I would not want to be in his shoes having to make those decisions all the time. I have come to respect the fact that, on these matters, he knows more than I do.

Kevin and I never had any problems working together. I love him to death and he loves me the same way. I've stayed at his house, I'm close with his kids, and we all play golf together. (Now that the kids are older, they beat us because we're both bad golfers . . . I just handle it better than Kevin does.) I'm like an uncle to his kids. Kevin still talks about Louie whenever we see each other. They were good friends. He thanks Louie for all the time they spent together and for helping him with his family.

The relationship between Vince, Kevin, and me is simple: we believe in each other and we respect each other. People in the business are sometimes so set in their ways that they have difficulty working with Kevin because he's always growing and expanding *his* way of thinking. More often than not, Kevin is the voice of reason balancing out our old-school ideas.

It's not fun to be told we can't do business like that anymore, but that's the way it is. When people tell me wrestling is not what it used to be, I tell them they're right . . . *It's better.*

Not that we can't improve even more in the future.

You have no idea how many times Kevin saved Vince and me from ourselves.

We were a team: I was wrestling; Kevin was producing; and Vince had the overall vision of where he wanted the whole product to go. We found connecting points between all of it, together, as a team.

Kevin has thanked me for helping him fit in and treating him like one of the boys. It was not always easy on him, back when his dad brought him to work at television tapings in Allentown. I didn't know we would become such good friends, but I'm glad we did. I thank him too for all he did for me as well.

In the old days, when we were having late-night working sessions at Vince's home, his little daughter, Stephanie, would sit on my lap as we put the television tapings or the next *WrestleMania* together. Before going to bed, she would come in to say goodnight and give both Vince and me a hug. I felt like a part of the family, like the friend turned into the cool uncle. Strangely enough, I've read on the internet that I am Stephanie's godfather. Let me get the record straight here: that's not true. People, don't go believing everything you hear about my life and career on the internet . . . At least not without checking with me first. Linda texted me a few nights ago because she had made my favorite cake for a family dinner and it made them think about me. It felt good to get that message.

I never really worked directly with Stephanie or Shane because as they were getting more involved, I was becoming less a part of the day-to-day operations. There was another rumor that I quit the business in 2004 as Triple H (Paul Levesque) was starting to assume more responsibilities. Now that's complete bullshit. Believe me when I write this: I was burned out at the time. And it was probably the third or fourth time I quit. (I've lost count.) No, I don't want Paul to fail. In fact, the opposite is true: I desperately want him to succeed. I want the business to continue to thrive after I'm gone, and after Vince is gone. Paul knows he's now part of my family. He knows, because I've said to him, "I'm not looking for a job, but if I can ever help you with anything, just ask and I will be there. I will be there for you, just like I was with Vince and his dad. You will always get the truth out of me."

So, yes, I let him do his thing. I can't be in his ear all the time and expect him to learn, grow, and create his own legacy. I believe he's doing a great job at finding his own way. We've texted about how highly I think of the NXT talent in Orlando. He tells me that Vince often brings up my name during meetings. It's fun to hear, and in a way I'm not surprised. I'm flattered that Paul now considers me family as well.

Back in the day, Vince and I would sometimes sit in silence across from each other for over half an hour, neither of us able to get a story moving for the Superstars. But that's the creative process for you: a lot of downtime. For me, that was the worst. When it happened,

Vince and I would start to get on each other's nerves. Without noticing, I would start to shake my legs. Vince would ask me to stop. After two or three times, I would say, "Yeah, but half an hour ago, you were the one shaking." We were pushing each others' buttons.

Very recently, we were finishing a meeting at a television taping when he started bouncing his leg up and down. I just looked at him funny. He started laughing right away, because he knew what I was thinking. We have probably spent way too much time together!

I never really fought Vince over anything. He's the boss. Sometimes I've been disappointed when I've felt strongly about something and I could not get Vince on board — but that's what happens in any job. It was never personal. In the end, it's his vision, and it's impossible for him to see things exactly like me. When it's all said and done, he has the final word. I'm the lucky one allowed to play in *his* sandbox. I often explain it this way: he likes chocolate ice cream and I like vanilla. He's my boss and I can't force-feed him vanilla. But I can attempt to convince him to try it. If he still wants his chocolate, I will have to find some and deliver it to him. There is a way to work with your boss without getting into a fight, and we've been much more productive that way. I don't remember him losing his cool even once in public. I saw him get angry only once and it had nothing to do with the business.

You see, Vince has a soft side that not a lot of people get to see, especially today. Back in the day, he threw a pool party at his home with more than forty guests from the company to celebrate Howard Finkel's birthday. He had a band, waiters, catering — the whole nine yards. At some point, people started to push each other into the pool with their clothes on. When I saw that, I decided to beat everyone to the punch and went inside, stripped down to my underwear, and jumped in. Bruce Prichard picked up my clothes and threw them in the pool: it was on. Alfred Hayes was next in . . . and pretty soon everyone but Vince was soaked. He wasn't happy his party had taken this turn.

You know who finally got Vince in the pool that day? Louie.

Like I said, Vince never gets mad to the point of making a scene or anything. I think it's part of the reason for his success, that he keeps his emotions under control. I remember a time when something particularly bad made it on TV, and he said, "Goddamn it, how stupid *are we*? How come no one said anything before we put that on the air?"

I said, "No one wants to tell you how wrong you are." I can't write here what he said next — but that's pretty much it as far as Vince getting mad.

The best part of our relationship? Even when things are bad, we have fun.

Bobby Heenan is another great wrestling mind. We're great friends; I loved him since Minneapolis where he was my manager. We shared rooms and traveled together for years. There are a lot of stories I could tell about Bobby. When we entered a hotel room, he would carry me in his arms as if we were newlyweds. We had fun laughing about that all the time. It was our thing. My favorite Bobby Heenan memory took place in Toronto. He'd had a few too many at the bar and I had to convince him to go back to the room and go to bed. Ten minutes later, I couldn't sleep so I started getting dressed to go out.

"Where are you going?" Bobby asked.

"I need to get out of this damn room, Bobby. I need some fresh air."

He said OK, but in his head I guess he thought that I wanted to pick someone up at the bar. All I really wanted was a few more drinks with the guys. I knew Bobby wouldn't sleep while waiting for me to return — he was just too curious. When I came back, it was pitch black. I made just enough noise and talked as if I had someone with me. "Shhh, he's asleep. Don't worry; we'll have a good time."

The following day when I told Bobby I was alone, we laughed again.

"Pat, I was sure you had someone with you. I didn't know how I was supposed to position myself. I didn't know if I could watch or not. You had me all screwed up in my mind."

He told that story again and again in the dressing room. We've had quite a few laughs about that night.

One time when Hogan was just hitting his peak, the agents' reports from the road were all about how great they were doing. I told Vince we'd made good soup . . . but the agents were the ones who were enjoying our recipe.

Around the same time, we had a show at the Meadowlands in New Jersey, not too far from the office. Vince told me we would not be working that Saturday because he had a wedding to attend. A lightbulb went off in my head.

"I'm going to the Meadowlands to have some fun."

I had one hell of an idea for the show and Vince was excited as I told him about it.

"You're going to have one hell of a time putting that together."

"Oh yeah, we'll tear the goddamn house down, Vince."

Then he started to throw in his own two cents for me to execute at the show within my idea. At first, it was cool, but then things kept evolving to the point that it was not really my idea anymore. I told him to call the agents and explain the idea himself, because I was not going anymore. He'd taken the fun out of it.

I wanted to speak to the talent face-to-face, not just make decisions in the office with him. But Vince is very creative, too, so much so that, I swear, sometimes I thought we'd drive each other crazy. Maybe he did drive me crazy? I don't know.

The part of my job I really loved back then, and still love today, is helping the talent directly with their matches. I learn more about them as people, and I become a better judge of who is worth sticking with by connecting with them at that level.

When Shawn Michaels and Marty Jannetty were first coming in, they were fired almost on the spot after destroying a hotel room. Vince was clear: "The Rockers are dead to me, Patrick." They had been there for a cup of tea, and no one knew Shawn would become the star he was destined to be. They were just new talents who had screwed up and made the company look bad. In Vince's mind, they had blown it and that was it.

I knew they had skills, and that they were just kids trying to entertain themselves. Kind of like me in a way. I never got in trouble like that, but I had wild parties on the road in my day. So periodically, I approached Vince with the idea of bringing them back. One day, he finally relented. "Call them, but it's on you. Make sure they behave this time."

I helped Shawn Michaels, but he was not the only one. I believed in Bret Hart as well, because I truly thought getting behind him was best for the whole company. I've never wanted to take credit for what they achieved, but since they have both said I was important in their career publicly, I guess I can acknowledge I helped. I would never brag about it to either of them when I was fighting for them to get a chance in the main event. The reason I fought for them was for the company and not for them personally. I thought it was good for business to have Shawn Michaels and Bret Hart as our top stars, because they were so very talented. There was no other reason. It's the same thing today when I put my two cents in about talent I feel can do more for us. In the end, the office always makes the final decision, and I just play a small part in the process. Vince *should get* all the credit for putting André and Hogan together. So today I think it can be told that I deserve a lot of credit for putting Shawn and Bret together.

But they're not the only ones I took an interest in. Vince didn't take me seriously when I first suggested Rey Mysterio for the main event of *WrestleMania 22*.

"Vince, the fans will never believe the kid has a chance for the championship. We work to get that reaction. People pop a nut when something unexpected like that happens. This will be a priceless moment, one you can't buy. Think about it, will you?"

By that time, I just knew when an idea had registered with him — and that day it did. He didn't change his mind right away, mind you, but the seed was planted and he came to the same conclusion I did. There was no need to fight for it — just wait and let him make the call.

I never told Rey it was my idea, but he was shocked when he finally learned the role I played. He made a point to thank me and he even mentioned it in his book. (Did everyone write a book before me?)

Daniel Bryan: could you imagine if he had *not* been brought back to WWE? When I tried to get his name back in discussions, Vince resurrected the "dead to me" line. Bryan had choked ring announcer Justin Roberts with his tie, unknowingly breaking company policy of choking anyone on television. I told Vince that many people had done a lot worse than Bryan, and they'd been brought back. Everyone makes mistakes. I thought we should give him another chance and John Cena even agreed with me. That didn't hurt. Bryan never asked me for anything; I just felt we should give him a second chance.

Just like I'd battled for Shawn, I refused to let go. When Bryan came back, he went over like there was no tomorrow. Because he's special. Look at all he's accomplished.

I've often told Vince, "It's hard for me sometimes. And I want you to understand something. I have two hats here: the friend and the colleague. Sometimes, it's difficult to be both at once. Don't get mad at me when I need to tell you the stuff you don't want to hear. Understand also that I will never abuse our friendship and tell you to do something that's not to better the business." You just can't use a man for your own personal gain and call him your friend. I will never do that, and I never have. Business is business and friendship is friendship. When I wasn't around in-person, Vince was always calling me. I think we needed to be friends to maintain our sanity — I was with him twenty-four hours a day — but business always came first.

Another talent I love is Chris Jericho. A few years back, when *NXT* first started, they wanted him to compete with one of the rookies from the show. He was a bit upset and he wanted to speak to me about it.

"Pat, you know I respect you. Tell me the truth. What do you think?"

"What's the problem?"

"I don't understand . . . It's not helping me."

"Chris, when he beats you, you'll go crazy. He got a lucky win on you . . . It's not going to kill you, it's just . . . entertainment."

The last time he came back to work with a big contract, I teased him.

"I'm so glad you came back. That loss, I guess it didn't kill your business."

He never forgot that lesson and he even mentioned the story in his third book. (Three books — I can barely get through one. Kids today . . .)

He's a hardworking son of a bitch. Guys his size have to be really good and produce every single time they go out there. I feel a real connection to this type of talent. They remind me of my own career; they face the same issues that I faced. Like me, they have something different from larger-than-life characters like Hulk Hogan, Randy Savage, or Ultimate Warrior.

What you project as a character is what ultimately sells tickets. Mickey Mouse still sells tickets for Walt Disney. It's almost as if Vince looked at wrestling years ago and decided to create something similar. He saw wrestling like the world of Disney, with all those characters aiming to be bigger than life. I never asked if that was his intention, and at some point we probably tried to do too much . . . Like making a garbage man a character and stuff like that, where everyone was cartoonish. I think we've struck a better balance today; there will always be a need for good characters, which can turn around the career of a good wrestler. Sure, we have hits and misses, but for every Duke "the Dumpster" Droese, there is an Undertaker.

You know, we weren't sure what to do with Undertaker when he first came to WWE.

"You know how I see him?" I said to Vince. "I'm not sure what is the exact word for it, but he reminds me of characters in old Western movies . . . That guy with the long black coat who would have different roles in town. Like a doctor . . ."

Vince said, "You're not describing a doctor, Patrick."

"I don't know what they are called."

Someone said, "From your description, I think you mean an undertaker."

That was a good name — I had the concept in my mind but I didn't know what to call it. The funny thing after that is when Percy Pringle came in to work for us, he told us he was a licensed mortician. Undertaker and Percy knew each other from Texas — it was a match made in hell. When the man who would become Paul Bearer said mortician, Vince and I started laughing. He was mortified, the poor soul. He was sure he had just blown his interview by saying the wrong thing. We reassured him he had said just the right thing. Isn't that amazing?

For a long time, it was only me working with Vince. Now, there are something like twenty people working in creative with him. How they get anything done amazes me.

I went years without seeing Hulk Hogan after he left Florida, but you could tell he was already starting to piece things together. He was always a Vince McMahon Jr. guy, part of his vision all along. I told Hulk to call Vince Jr. when we crossed paths working in Montréal for André's promotion. The rest, as they say, is history.

In this business, if you love what you do, all you have to do is invest in some boots and a pair of tights. That's what Hogan did, and he became bigger than all of us. His success then trickled down to everyone else in the business.

I believed in Hulk Hogan as "our guy" in the mid-1980s. He was *the* hero and we depended on him. All that mattered was that he was WWE's locomotive. When we worked together, it was my job as a producer to make him comfortable and let him know that the company had his back. That didn't mean, however, I would not poke fun at him.

On one occasion, he was in a big meeting with Vince in one of the boardrooms, so I went to the top of the tower in Stamford and hung a Hogan wrestling buddy from the roof so that it would dangle just in front of the window. We all had a good laugh, and that's all that mattered. You need to laugh in this business if you want to make it. Too bad it's not always fun. It can be very hard and there is often not enough time to enjoy success.

And when tragedy strikes there is even less time to pick yourself up.

13
GOODBYE, MY FRIEND

"But through it all, when there was doubt,
I ate it up and spit it out"

It wasn't always fun and I wasn't always laughing, though I tried. I fired someone once after a particularly bad screwup, and he called me an no-good Irish motherfucker. There might have been a gay slur thrown in there somewhere as well. I went to Vince's office and blew a gasket. "It's not true, Vince, and it really pisses me off. *I'm not Irish.*"

But, seriously, I had to go through some dark times. There was absolutely no laughter associated with the sexual harassment scandal. In the wake of other individuals' misconduct within the company, I was wrongly accused of being involved in their inappropriate conduct. The fact that I was gay certainly played a part in me being targeted like that. Out of loyalty, I decided to make life easy on Vince: I quit the company. In my mind, that was it; I was done. I was out of the business and I needed a new job. I even went to school to become a bartender. I figured that if I was good enough, I could work in an airport or something and still meet people from all over the world. It was weird being out of the business completely. I really don't want to go into the details, or give publicity to people who don't deserve it, but this is my book and I need to make this statement to clarify things forever.

I understand that no matter what I say about the situation, people are going to believe what they'll believe. (And that's why I've decided not to labor over the details.) I could spend page after page on the whole story of going to civil court against that no-good son of a bitch . . . To this day, I honestly don't know why he picked on me. I talked to him twice while he worked for WWE.

I said hello to him and welcomed him to the company shortly after he was hired, and I told him he would have a good time working with us. I didn't see him for quite a while after that. He worked in our studio facility and I was at the tower. We were in two different buildings.

I remember the only other time I met him was when Vince had asked me to come to his office. Before you enter, there's a waiting room. He was there, waiting to see Vince as well. I said hi to him and went in to speak with Vince. I spoke with Vince for maybe five minutes at most. Then, right after seeing me, Vince fired the guy. I honestly didn't know that's why he was waiting. In fact, I only found out he had been let go two weeks later. I had not even seen his work on television. It took him six months after being fired to bring the allegations forward, and it was coincidence that that's when everything else hit the media. It was fucking awful.

Quitting WWE over all of that was the worst time for me professionally. It was horrible. I was loyal, but I was also heartbroken because there was really nothing I could do but wait for my name to be cleared. I was at the mercy of one man's lies just because I was gay. Worse, some people I considered friends, whom I had helped in the business, went on television and blatantly lied about me.

I later learned that Vince hired an outside agency, the Fairfax Group, to perform an independent internal investigation to determine if I had been guilty of *anything*. I understood why the company needed to do that. I had quit not because I was guilty, but because I didn't want to put the company through an ordeal. The investigators talked to everyone: from referees to production crew, from the talent to the office staff. Anyone and everyone who might have had to deal with me in any capacity.

Finally, Vince asked me to come to his office. And this is what he said, "Pat, you could run for President of the United States and you'd be elected. Not one person that we interviewed had a bad word to say about you. Please come back to work."

I was ecstatic. I returned to the company for *SummerSlam 1992* in England; I was *not* secretly working for the company as some have suggested. And, as I just told you, I really was planning to become a bartender. It was such a relief when I got back to work. Everyone was happy to see me — I can't even count how many hugs I received. It felt very good to be back, but still the whole experience was just horrible, and it hurt.

If I had wanted it, I could have pursued a big offer to go to WCW. I received word that they wanted to speak with me. I let them know through the same channels that there was no point in talking, as I would never even entertain the idea. It never crossed my mind to work elsewhere in the business, even after I resigned. I was loyal to the company and Vince as if I were his father. It was never about money or glory.

Another thing I want to say is that I've never given steroids to anyone. I resent that anyone would say that about me. There is one Montreal journalist that went on the radio and said I distribute steroids out of my suitcase or something like that. My brothers and sisters heard that, and it hurt them. It didn't bother me the same way; I was not living in Montréal. But I had to go through all of that bullshit with my family for no good reason because of these gratuitous accusations.

When I decided to resign, Louie was disgusted that I'd been dragged through all of this mud. He was behind me 100 percent and he knew I was innocent. He was my rock.

I've never been accused of breaking any law in court, never been found guilty of anything. But still those allegations haunt me because they're repeated by people who don't bother to check the facts. Through it all, three decades later, nobody has ever come forward or even insinuated that I did something wrong to them at any point in time. It was just crazy shit people made up because they were mad at the company. I am gay, and because of that I became an easy target.

Let me just say to end this: if you didn't get to WWE, or didn't succeed, it was because you were not good enough. And not because of anything I did, or didn't do.

―――――――――――――――――――――

When you first start wrestling, you don't make money. And when you finally start making some, you want to improve your life with the big house and the big car. Then one day, maybe, you realize that you don't need all that shit. You start making smart choices, like getting a smaller place and taking care of your money. Louie and I bought a humongous house in Connecticut: 5,000 square feet and 171 windows (and not one of them was identical). Then one day I woke up and realized I needed that as much as I needed another hole in my head. When I tried to hire someone to wash all of those windows, I was quoted $8,000. Seriously. It was in a neighborhood with big houses and people with a lot of money, so that's the price everyone was paying. It was crazy to me. I'm not paying $8,000 to have you wash my windows even if there are 171 of them. You know what he said? "It's 171, outside *and* inside."

I still said no and I realized I needed to sell that place. I found a handyman who did the job for $150, proving that it was a completely ridiculous price the specialist had quoted me. You always think you can afford the big house, but it makes no sense. Once you have it, you don't want it anymore. The best two days I had with that place were the day we bought it and the day we sold it.

Through it all, Louie and I were together. We were a couple for forty years. When the AIDS epidemic hit, we decided to be completely exclusive. We were aware of the dangers of the spread of the disease and we didn't waste time making that decision. I trusted him and he trusted me. We were smart and we wanted to enjoy life. We could travel and go anywhere — why risk that?

And that's part of why I was so devastated when I lost him.

I was working in Pittsburgh at the *King of the Ring* PPV on June 28, 1998. It was a night made famous for the Hell in a Cell match between Mick Foley and Undertaker. Louie was at his sister's place, just outside of Boston. I was supposed to go back to Montréal after the show. Louie was going to join me, and we were going to spend a week at home with my family.

I got the emergency call while in a meeting at the arena.

When I was told that Louie had passed away, it was like I'd been shot. A part of me died that day, too.

Linda McMahon sat with me; she held me and gave me a handkerchief. She took care of me and led me to a small room, so I could be in private. "Just sit here and relax, Pat," she said. Then Vince came in, and even in the midst of the craziness that is a WWE PPV day, he stopped to be with me and say, "I'm so sorry for your loss, Pat. We'll take care of everything."

About an hour after I'd gotten the news, a limousine was waiting to take me back to the hotel. Linda said, "Take your time at the hotel, pack your bag, and compose yourself. We will have a jet ready for you to go to be with Louie's family."

She joined me at the hotel and brought me some vodka. I had a drink or two. Then they had me driven to the airport. When I got to Boston, another limo was waiting. I got there at 3 a.m. and all of Louie's family was there for me.

It was his second heart attack. This one came very suddenly, out of nowhere. I was surprised since he seemed like he was in such good shape. He played golf all the time. I told him that eighteen holes were more than enough in one day, but some days he played thirty-six. As always, he told me not to tell him what to do.

I was lost without him. I wanted to let his family decide everything, but they insisted I make all the decisions. The worst part was seeing him in the casket.

Holy shit, that was tough.

Later on, after the close family had been by ourselves for a while, we started receiving friends and other family members. Then it hit us: there was a lineup outside. He came from a well-known family in his neighborhood; a lot of people wanted to pay their respects. And he was so well liked — he had made so many friends through the years. Everybody from the WWE office came. The priest said to his sister, "What did your brother do to draw all of these people?"

"He was just a good person," she said. And that was true.

I took very little time off. I was in shock, I guess. Vince said, "Best thing for you might just be to come back to work right away. Get your mind off it." I've never told that to anybody. But he was probably right.

The hard part came when I was alone at night in a hotel room. My reflex before going to bed had always been to call Louie. I'd reach for the phone. Then it would hit me all over again. He was gone. And I would cry like a baby. So I'd pick myself up quickly and go right back to the bar for a few more drinks with the guys before heading straight back up to bed. I'm used to it now, and after a little while, things became a bit easier. Still, it is the most difficult thing I ever lived through.

Louie had worked for WWE, in the merchandising department, for a little while, and he did very well at first. But the head of the department was not an easy fellow to get along with. Vince and Louie were very tight by that point, and one day they had a conversation where it was decided that it was probably better for Louie to stop working for the company. They never had any issues after that, and they always had fun together. Louie told him that the only thing he needed to change was that he should thank people more often.

"What the hell for? It's their job," Vince said.

"I know, Vince, but it never hurts to add a thank-you."

That was my Louie.

Vince has never forgotten it, to this day.

When my mother and father died, I was not the one in charge of making the important decisions. For Louie, I had to do everything, and I think it just made things even more difficult. I gave all of his jewelry, his clothes, and his golf clubs to his brothers. I didn't keep anything — I have my memories. In my wallet, I still have a small picture of Louie. I've had it since forever. I have another picture in my house in Florida and some on my phone. That's it.

It's hard now to return to an empty house. After a while, I needed to break away from the past, so I sold our place in Tampa. Now I have a place in Fort Lauderdale. Young or old, a relationship is not always about sex; it's about having someone to talk to, to kiss, to hold. I'm not sure if I could meet someone today and have a real, meaningful relationship. I'm not looking, that's for sure. If it happens, it happens. I bring my friends or my sister on cruises or trips now, just to have someone to share the experience, but if I'm alone that's all right, too.

I realized I experienced closure about two years ago. Mick Foley was the one who finally mustered the guts to ask me about that day. Louie's passing is one of the few things he remembers from the day of that match with Taker. He hugged me while his tooth still hung by his nose. (It's a wrestling thing, and you might not get it. But look it up on WWE Network.)

I had just started to talk openly about being gay and how difficult it is, still, to open up. Guys like Mick Foley always respected the fact that I was not fully comfortable talking about this with just anyone. But on that day, he finally said what was on his mind.

"Pat, can I ask you a question? When Louie died . . . He had his heart attack during *King of the Ring* . . . Did Louie die during my match?"

"Goddamn it, no, you crazy bastard. He died three hours before the show."

Mick was relieved. "So, I didn't kill Louie?"

He'd harbored that guilt for thirteen years. That day I laughed for the first time while speaking about losing Louie. I needed that. Mick, thank you, my friend.

So goodbye my friend
I know I'll never see you again
But the time together through all the years
Will take away these tears
It's okay now
Goodbye my friend

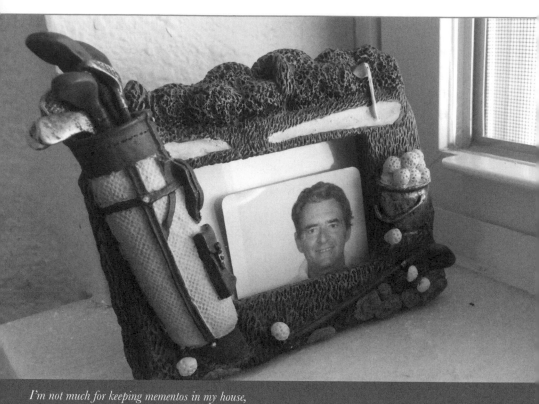

I'm not much for keeping mementos in my house,
but that frame with a golf bag is a daily reminder of my Louie.

WRESTLEMANIA, THE ROYAL RUMBLE, AND THE MONTRÉAL SCREWJOB

"And now, as tears subside, I find it all so amusing to think I did all that"

At *WrestleMania 29*, I hid in the crowd near the main camera. I've tried to do it every year since. Now don't go and look for me — it would ruin my ability to reflect and enjoy the event. I want to just feel the moment, and I got very emotional that first time. Right after the show started, I went backstage and straight up to Vince.

"I know you're busy, but I have to tell you something. I just came back from sitting in the crowd and it was so beautiful that I was crying."

He said something that made me cry all over again. "Patrick, you helped build this. Thank you."

Before anything else, I was a fan and a performer. How could I have imagined when I first left Montréal for Boston that I would find myself in a football stadium, five decades later, for a show like *WrestleMania*, in a promotion that I helped build? *WrestleMania 29* in New Jersey was a very emotional night. It scared me to think I might have spent all that time working in a factory in Montréal instead.

Referee for the main event of the first ever WrestleMania*!*

We don't work as closely now, but Vince and I will always have a special bond. Not that long ago, I was with Vince on the company's private plane and I was telling him how much I appreciated riding with him, but that maybe my place should go to someone who contributes more.

"You are where you belong," he said. "You helped build this place. Some people don't know how important you are. You mean a lot to me. It's really the other way around . . . If you were not with me on this plane, they should all be wondering, 'How come Pat is not with Vince?'"

It amazes me to think of all we've achieved on that private jet. Sometimes we'll land at 1 p.m. and two hours later we'll still be in there, talking about the old days. We still have a great time together. The limousine picks us up and brings us directly to the arena, and we do it all over again. That's how I like it. It always brings me back to a time when things were simpler.

Like the first *WrestleMania*. I was the referee for the first ever *WrestleMania* main event.

I have all the respect in the world for Muhammad Ali, but when he showed up to be the referee for that match between Hulk Hogan and Mr. T against Paul Orndorff and Roddy Piper, I realized right away that he would not be able to perform a normal referee's duties in the ring. Vince agreed and it was quickly decided that it would be my job. I had put the match together, and I could help if they needed it — and I could run interference if one of the guests felt a little bit too courageous. That might seem crazy today, but back then we were so secretive about everything that celebrities wanted to jump in on the action. In the end, when Ali jumped in the ring looking to fight, everyone was nervous. It was up to me to keep the peace. Piper needed to hit someone after losing, and I wound up being his victim. I was always ready to take one for the team, no matter the circumstance.

Billy Martin, the famous New York Yankees manager, was the ring announcer that day and he wanted to fight, too. I don't know what gets people going when they're watching the matches, but everyone thinks they can battle with the best of us.

At least Liberace and the Rockettes didn't want to rumble . . . And people from the office had a great time with all the celebrities at a private party at Rockefeller Center after the show. Simple pleasures, maybe, but it was still unbelievable for that little Montréal kid who moved to America with twenty dollars and a suitcase.

My mother would have been so proud — I was working with her hero.

Years ago, when my family got our first television, we put it on top of the refrigerator. It was never easy to watch something. With eleven of us, there was just not enough room. But one night a week, my mother had to be alone for a half hour — to watch Liberace in black and white. We all got out of the house. It was the least we could do for our mom. She was just madly in love with Liberace. Years later, in San Francisco, I was having breakfast one morning and reading the paper when I discovered an ad saying Liberace was going to be in town the next day.

I didn't say a word. I went downtown to the box office. There was a young girl behind the desk and I told her, "I'd like three front-row seats for Liberace."

"Sir, those tickets are gone."

"Don't tell me that. Come on, you've got to be able to do something."

There was a guy working in the box office who turned around at that point. He said, "Hey, Pat Patterson — what're you doing here?"

Working with Liberace at the first WrestleMania. *What a moment!*

"I really need to get three tickets in the front row."

"For you, we'll do it."

He gave me the tickets. When I got home, I told me my mom, who was in town with my dad, "Tonight we're going to see a special show, Mom. We're going to see Liberace."

I was choked up, you know? We're there in the front row, and when he came out, I mean, she was crying. Then the son of a bitch came over to the front row and grabbed my mom by the hand and kissed it.

Unbelievable. Simply unbelievable.

She'd never imagined something like that would happen to her and it's a great memory for me.

What a lot of people don't know about the first *WrestleMania* is exactly how much Vince gambled on that show. It was everything — and I really mean everything. I will always remember him saying, "If this doesn't work out, Patrick, we'll all have to find another job."

That made my small appearance at *WrestleMania XXX* even more special, as they decided to shoot a little salute to the first *WrestleMania*. I had a great line in the skit with Mean Gene and the four participants of the match. I came up with the line myself. "You want to fight? You're going to hurt each other!"

In 1996, I went into the WWE Hall of Fame, the same year as Killer Kowalski. Who would have thought that was possible when we were paired up in Australia as a tag team for the first time? Or when he signed my picture in the Forum dressing room? That's the journey life takes you on. Today the Hall of Fame ceremony is a much bigger event, broadcast all over the world on WWE Network. Back then, it was more intimate. Still, it meant the world to me.

When Burt Reynolds was at *WrestleMania X*, I personally walked behind him to make sure no one tried to pull his hair. I told Donald Trump about it, too. Fans can get crazy at times, and they might try to pull his hair. He thanked me for the advice. Celebrities generally can't imagine how out of hand things can get when our fans get really excited.

I was there when Lawrence Taylor was training for *WrestleMania XI*. He scared me because he wasn't afraid of trying anything — including jumping from the top rope. I told him he was going to break his leg or worse, but he told me not to worry. He was a natural, easy to work with, and a very good listener. I had a good time being the referee for his match against Bam Bam Bigelow. It's too bad about what's happened to LT since.

I will never forget the match Bret and Shawn had at *WrestleMania XII*. I was not working for WWE at the time   I was in the midst of one of my many retirements — but Vince told me I needed to come and watch *WrestleMania* in person.

"What's the main event?"

"Bret versus Shawn, Iron Man."

"I'll be there."

That match was my idea, but what I like most is that they tore the house down. It's nothing less than what I expected them to do, and I cried watching them. This is exactly the type of match I would have loved to perform on a stage like *WrestleMania*.

People can say what they want about wrestling, but to us, it's real. The performance, the pressure — it's all real. So when you accomplish something like the main event of *WrestleMania*, it conjures up

In 1996, I was inducted in the WWE Hall of Fame —
the same year as my idol Killer Kowalski.

real emotions. *WrestleMania VI* was in such a big building, Toronto's
SkyDome (now the Rogers Centre), that after the show we actually
could not find Ultimate Warrior. There are different dressing rooms
everywhere in that building, and no one could figure out where
the hell he was. We were screaming our lungs out looking for him.
Finally, we opened this door that we figured was probably a broom
closet or something. He was in there, sitting by himself in the dark,
crying with the championship on his lap.

"Are you OK?" I asked.

"Pat, I can't believe how you guys took care of me."

"It's OK, take your time, I understand. Just wanted to check and
make sure you were all right."

I had been crying earlier myself in the crowd with Vince, watching
Ultimate Warrior's match against Hogan, as our vision came to life.

It's the same in any form of live entertainment, I figure. Let's say you're Frank Sinatra and you give it all you've got and tear the house down . . . When you get back in the dressing room, you don't want to be bothered. You don't want to talk. You just want to feel it, inside of you, for as long as possible.

Not finding guys for up to an hour after big matches happens more than you think — they need time alone to let their emotions out. It's hard because we're supposed to be tough guys, but the business generates a lot of emotions in us.

And that's as real as it gets.

When I had a match like that, I just could not sleep afterward; there was just too much adrenaline coursing through me. The emotions carried me all night. I would relive it in my mind over and over again. I wanted to party and have fun while letting it sink in forever. If only you could experience it the way we do, you would see what we do in a completely different light.

But the crowds, the fans, are always a part of it. Once you hook the people, once they're happy, they give you so much energy. That's why I loved performing — it's something that's almost impossible to explain.

It's the same thing when the show doesn't go as you might have hoped — you can't sleep either. But that's how you learn and get better.

When I give ideas to guys today, I visualize myself doing what I've suggested in the ring. When they go out there and make it come to life, it's just as if I'd been in there myself, just like for the match between Shawn and Bret I mentioned earlier.

I remember a thing or two about other big shows, like *Survivor Series* and the *Royal Rumble* as well.

Chuck Norris enjoys a kind of cult popularity today because of those cute jokes about how tough he is. My favorite is "They once made a Chuck Norris toilet paper, but it wouldn't take shit from any-body." That's pretty much his whole gimmick now. Back in 1994, he did *Survivor Series* for WWE as a ringside enforcer. He was at the height of his *Walker, Texas Ranger* popularity. Let me tell you, he was so nervous. Celebrities were never sure whether the wrestlers would play along or, in his case, try to test his tough-guy persona.

"Don't worry, I'm Pat Patterson; I will take care of everything," I said.

And you know what he said? "I'm Chuck Norris and I trust you." Ain't that something?

Somebody should put that on the internet: "When Chuck Norris gets nervous, he trusts Pat Patterson."

Everything went as planned: Jeff Jarrett took a big fall for him and everyone was happy.

I used to love to sit at the bar and have a drink with the talent. Bret was one of my favorites. He was not a big drinker, but we would talk about the business, family, or what was going on in the news. I became real close to him and considered him a friend.

When the Montréal Screwjob happened in 1997, they made sure I wasn't in the know, because I would have tried to find a way to talk Vince out of it. The issues between Bret and Vince had run deep. I was never consulted and, in hindsight, that's probably for the best. It bothered me because it was two guys I cared for over the years. But Shawn was a little bastard back then, and Bret was as stubborn as only Bret Hart can be. I think they both look back at it now and realize how foolish it all was.

To make a long story short, Vince decided to take the championship away from Bret without telling him. When I found out about it, I was so angry that I wanted to quit. I was in gorilla (that's what we call the place where Vince and all the producers sit during the matches, named after my friend Gorilla Monsoon). It's funny now, though it wasn't at the time. Everyone who knew what was going to happen took off just before the end of the match; I was suddenly . . . alone. Anyway, I stood my ground because I needed to be there for Bret. I remember thinking: *He's going to nail me, and if he nails me, he nails me.* I was face-to-face with him as he came through the curtain. Right away, I said, "Bret, I had nothing to do with that. It was fucking news to me."

He just kept walking.

I was furious, and I really couldn't believe what had just happened. I grabbed my briefcase, I went down to the arena garage, got in my car, went to the hotel, and ordered a cocktail. In my mind, I said that's it. I'm going to quit the business. I got another drink. And then the more I thought about it, the more I figured I looked like a guy who ran away. I went back to the building and up the escalator. Backstage was almost all empty. I asked a security guard, "Where's Bret?"

"He's down in the locker room."

"I'm going in."

"Pat, you shouldn't go in there."

"Why shouldn't I?"

"Vince got into it, and Bret hit Vince."

"I don't care, I'm going. If he has to hit me, let him hit me."

I knocked on the door and asked to come in. They opened the door and I walked in. I grabbed his hand, and I said, "Bret, look me in the eyes. I'm looking at you. All the work we did together, I've helped you, and I really respect you. I swear to you I had nothing to do with this goddamn thing and that I didn't know. So please, if you believe me, shake my hand."

He wouldn't shake my hand. I said OK and then I left.

That went on for a long time.

For years, he was sure I was in on it. Everybody trusted me, so I felt really bad, and I wanted to help fix things.

Bret Hart is a special talent, and we have a special bond from sharing the same passion for our business.

All the wrestlers trusted me even though I worked for the office. I would always try to find a solution that made everyone happy. I guess I was just . . . patient. Behind all that posturing and jockeying for position was a bunch of insecure performers. I decided to never let myself be afraid that someone was going to have a better idea than me. I want the best idea possible for the show, and everyone I worked with seemed to appreciate that.

Bret was angry at everyone and especially with the company. Every year at the Cauliflower Alley Club in Las Vegas, I would say hi to him, and he would be polite, but not very vocal, and we would never really hang the way we used to. The weird thing is, I felt like I let Bret *and* Vince down. In the end, I needed to smooth things over between the two sides.

Finally, in Las Vegas one year, I pulled Bret aside in a hotel staircase.

"Would you fucking wake up you, stubborn son of a bitch?! I'm sick of it. We were so close, and you still give me the cold shoulder every time we meet. You're just being stubborn now, because you know I had nothing to do with that night. Stop playing games. Give me a hug and shake my hand."

I was so happy he did.

I also asked if he'd mind if I talked to Vince about him.

"Pat, Vince would never take me back."

"Are you kidding? You can still do many things; you have a big following. Unlike you, I don't know what Vince thinks, let me mention it to him."

I simply told Vince that I'd made up with Bret and explained that I thought maybe he could be an asset to us, instead of an enemy. I reminded him he was still hot as a firecracker in Europe (and he still is to this day).

"Patrick, I don't want to dig up all that stuff again, not today."

"Still, it's something to think about."

The next thing I knew, *big surprise*, Kevin Dunn and Vince had set up a meeting with Bret. They wanted me to come. I said, "No, you guys take care of your business; mine is done." When they came back, they had a deal for Bret to return.

Why did I bother? Because I care. I see them so miserable over a match and I can't help myself. You should only be allowed to be angry for six months over a goddamn match, right? But after that, get over it. There is no point in staying mad for years, don't you think?

That Montréal fiasco was very strange, even for this business, and in this case Bret had good reason to be angry — just not forever. I'm glad it's behind us, but what were the odds of it happening in Montréal of all places, my hometown? Crazy.

The first *Royal Rumble* was on January 24, 1988, in Hamilton, Ontario. The difference between WWE's *Royal Rumble* and a traditional over-the-top rope battle royal is that the participants come into the match at two-minute intervals — not all at the same time at the beginning of the match. I wanted to create something special, something just like we had in San Francisco where it had been such a hot event.

The more I kept running the idea over in my mind, the more it took shape and I was sure I was on to something. I felt it: every instinct in my body told me it would work.

So I finally brought the idea to Vince. He laughed at the concept at first, saying that an hour was way too long to keep fans interested. I didn't get upset; I knew sometimes he needed time for ideas to sink in. But I made sure to say, "All right, but keep it in mind, will you? Because I know this can work."

Sometime later, we had a meeting with the USA Network about doing a special. We worked on the special with Dick Ebersol, who did the *Saturday Night Main Event* shows with us for NBC. It was going to be a three-hour live show, but it needed something to take it to the level of a *WrestleMania* or *Survivor Series*. In desperation, Vince threw my idea out there. "Pat, tell Dick about your stupid idea for that battle royal."

"First, it's not stupid. I think it's a good idea. Goddamn it, I think it's a *great* idea."

Ebersol loved the concept right away. He immediately imagined the drama of the clock ticking down onscreen and the audience's anxious anticipation of who was going enter the ring next being played out every two minutes.

"Vince, it's great TV," he said.

Vince told me to start putting it together, and I programmed the first *Rumble* all by myself. The final touches were completed at the arena on the morning of the show because I kept expecting Vince to give me some direction on where he wanted things to go. But he never did.

"It's your match," he told me when we got to the building.

We didn't want to simply call it a battle royal. We had people at the office who came up with names and they submitted something like fifty of them to us. As soon as we read "Royal Rumble," we knew we had the name. Personally, though, I didn't care what it was called: I just wanted to see my idea to come to life.

The talent was freaking out on the morning of the show because of all of my detailed instructions. None of them had ever done a match quite like this before. When it was all said and done, I think they loved it. I was happy, too.

The first *Royal Rumble* was a success, but until it was over, we didn't really know if it would work. I knew it was a unique idea, but until a crowd responds, it's hard to know for sure.

That first *Rumble* had only twenty participants; I feel that thirty is the ideal number. At times, the match has expanded to forty participants and it's been too many. You need to have main-event wrestlers in there, to really drive home the importance of the match, but people have to feel that just about anyone can win — just as was the case in 1992 when Ric Flair won the match *and* the vacant WWE Championship. That show took place in Albany, New York. When I came back to the locker room, Flair was crying like a little kid. He was so happy. "Thank you so much, you guys. Oh my God, I can't believe this is happening." Imagine a man that celebrated and decorated freaking out. It was one hell of a night.

I'm repeating myself here, but I don't care. People can say what they want about the business, but to us, the performers, it's as real as real can be. Ric had done everything that could be done in wrestling twice, but winning the WWE Championship in the *Royal Rumble* was *real* for him. Moments like that validate what we do. That's the passion I try to share with our Superstars today. You need to think about and believe in what you are going to do out there to make it special.

Some friends of mine tell me that their kids, who are into WWE Superstars today, love watching classic *Royal Rumble* matches on WWE Network and that they don't care if they don't know all the characters. They still find the match interesting and surprising. In a way, most of the *Royal Rumble* matches have, in this manner, passed the test of time. They are like a good movie you can watch over and over again. It has now become WWE's second biggest event of the year, and I believe it's going to remain there forever.

Now, if I could just get a few more of my ideas in before I go . . .

You know what I would like to see done every year? I'd love to be introduced as the creator of the match and give a cup to the winner at ringside. It would be just like the Stanley Cup in hockey. You would have all the past winners' names on it and people could look for the names of their favorite Superstars on there. The winner could celebrate by drinking champagne from it. (We would need to go back in time and have the winner of every edition of the match engraved on it.) People could get their picture taken with the Cup when we do Fan Axxess at *WrestleMania*. You could sell replicas as well.

Maybe for the thirtieth anniversary in 2018? The Patterson Cup? What do you think?

FROM THE STOOGES
TO THE ROCK

"To say the things he truly feels;
And not the words of one who kneels."

When my in-ring career was over, I accepted it. When I was called upon to perform as one of "the stooges" with Gerald Brisco during the Attitude Era, I wasn't too crazy about the idea of coming out of retirement. I've only recently realized how popular that bullshit we did was. We even made a cameo appearance at *WrestleMania 31* reprising our roles. People loved it, I guess — they talk to me about it all the time.

At the time, all I could see was how far I was from what I used to be. I was a main-event wrestler and I used to draw thousands of people; I was never comic relief. It was a hard pill to swallow — that this was all I could do to contribute. But it's remembered fondly, and a lot of people were watching. And the truth is, we were funny. And Brisco and I had great chemistry. Still, I hated it back then. That wasn't the real performer in me out there. It was OK, I guess, but it was cartoonish. I could not imagine Lou Thesz or Buddy Rogers

Gerald Briscoe and I had great chemistry as Vince's Stooges.

doing what we were doing, and that's how I wanted to be remembered. I did make a few bucks out of it, however. Today, I see it a bit differently. People appreciate and respect the performance while understanding the limitations of our age.

We did draw an 8.1 rating for our match against the Mean Street Posse on *Raw* in 1999, not bad when you think about it. I did the best I could with it, but I still wish I could have been young enough to play with those main-event performers on WWE's stage. I would have loved to work with Hogan, Macho Man, Stone Cold, Shawn, Bret, Triple H, and The Rock. We would have played to sold-out arenas in my prime. The fact that I won the Hardcore Championship in the midst of that run meant very little to me. (Even if I was the oldest champion of any kind in WWE history.) I just don't think that way.

The stooges was . . . what it was. Gerald was always checking how our segment did in the ratings, or on who we would be working with on a show. He brings up our record rating all the time — ask him about it. First and foremost, I was afraid of being hurt. Being in the ring with all those young kids eager to make an impression was not always easy, and I was no spring chicken. It was fun to go up against Shane and Vince, however, and it was something people wanted to see. But let's be serious for a minute — the whole thing is crazy to even think about. I was in a match with Stone Cold Steve Austin. It was not the main event, but not too bad for an older gentleman like me.

I especially loved to do backstage vignettes with The Rock, because it was both fun and good television.

But I just don't see things like a lot of people. I never thought, "Oh my God, I'm working with the biggest star in the business." I didn't even think *Damn, he's the son of my good friend.*

Business came first. And sometimes, in our business, little things just happened on camera and those moments are magical. I didn't care about the stooges while doing it, and I always blame Vince for the idea . . . So I will also give him the credit for anything about the whole thing that was good, including the ratings we achieved.

I am so fortunate to have seen so many countries while being paid to travel. I've always resolved to live my life to the fullest, so I took time to enjoy and experience those visits. I didn't spend all of my time at the hotel or at the arena. We went to Paris, and I was in charge of the show, which seems impossible to me when I travel back in time to watch myself lacing up my first pair of boots. That was special in a way that's hard to explain: making it in France has always meant something unique to a French Canadian because that's where all of us Quebecers originally came from.

One night, we were in a great little town in the north of France. We were staying in a wonderful hotel and had an afternoon show. After some sightseeing, I asked if they had a karaoke bar in town. I went back to the hotel, ate something, had a couple of drinks at the bar, and told some of the guys I was going to the karaoke bar to sing. A few guys joined me. The place was small and didn't look promising. Then suddenly, the whole crew appeared and we took over the place, having a blast, singing until closing time. Everybody sang — even Titus O'Neil. He was great. And a much better dancer than me.

The following day, we were headed to Amsterdam, but only for a night. I'd never been there before, and we were staying at a hotel forty minutes from downtown. I told myself to go out; I might never come back. It was cool — everyone was mellow in that country. I went to the Red Light District and everything, and that brought back memories. Back in the days when I was out on the road full-time, we once ran a show in Marseille. They had a famous Red Light District and many of the guys wanted to see it after the show. I was in charge and I said no. "No one goes out tonight. We have an early plane in the morning."

I'd gone in the afternoon with Miss Elizabeth and some of the other women because they wanted to see it, too. On one side of the street there were girls; on the other side there were guys available. When the girls told the boys about that, everybody wanted to go. And that's why I said no. Because I knew I'd be missing three or four wrestlers in the morning, and there were no mobile phones back then to track someone quickly.

Another time, on a tour of Ireland, two stars who shall remain nameless were arrested. We were in one of the nicest hotels we've ever booked. They had a bar in the lobby just for the people staying there, which was perfect for us to unwind in and not be bothered by anyone. There was also a nightclub in the basement that was open to everyone. People staying in the hotel could go in without having to wait in line. The line outside to get in was a few blocks long. After two hours, the booze started to talk and some people began testing the wrestlers. One of the top stars . . . told them off. I tried to calm him and another wrestler down and bring everyone upstairs to the other bar, so that no one would bother us. Sadly I had no success.

I told the two men not to get in trouble and I left.

I guess what had to happen happened. They got into a fight; they went to jail. I was in charge of the tour so the police called me in the morning to ask if I wanted to come and get my friends.

"No, let them take care of their own business."

It was always a pain in the ass on European tours — getting guys up and on time for the bus so we could make the next town or take the next plane sometimes seemed impossible. I had to pinch myself on many mornings; it was as if I was working with Ray Stevens all over again. Incredibly, I've had to help guys pack their bags and, occasionally, even help them get dressed. The worst case of all happened in Belgium.

I was napping on the second floor of the hotel. Everyone in the hallways around me was politely speaking French when suddenly I heard someone screaming, in English, "You motherfucker, you piece of shit." It had to be one of my guys. I went downstairs in my bare feet.

One of our most popular tag-team wrestlers, who shall also remain nameless, was cursing the front-desk clerk, holding him by his tie, because they couldn't dial home. Steve Lombardi had come down as well, and he was able to calm the guys after telling them that he would go to their room and show them how to telephone home from Europe. The poor clerk could not understand what they were saying because he didn't speak any English. As I was going back to my room, guess who came out of the elevator covered in blood? Another wrestler, of course.

"What happened to you?"

"Nothing."

Nothing, my ass. He had gotten into a fight with someone who worked for WWE behind the scenes. Everything that could go wrong in that hotel went wrong. A few people even had to be let go when we came back from that tour in the late 1980s.

Being the boss on those trips was never fun.

Of course, not everything was tragic on tour. One night in France, we were in a town called *Clermont*, ironically. It was our last night in Europe and it was far from a full house. So I told the talent to keep the show moving, since we had an early flight in the morning. "Let's get out of here healthy and quickly," I said.

Before the main event, Bret Hart didn't want to go out because they had played Macho Man's music instead of his. I insisted he had to go to the ring anyway. He wound up being a good sport about it, even impersonating Macho Man in the ring to make light of the situation. Now that was funny.

Today, the guys are a bunch of angels compared to when I was in charge of the tours. They all say "yes, sir" *and* they listen.

But the truth is we didn't need to be outside of North America for a situation to take a turn for the worse.

I guess some of you will want me to give you my take on the British Bulldogs' fight with the Rougeau brothers in the dressing room. Dynamite Kid had slapped Jacques Rougeau in the dressing room a few weeks earlier, accusing him of being about to stooge him off to the office. Back in those days, the wrestlers always found a way to get even when they felt disrespected in front of their peers.

Yes, I was there for the receipt. And let me tell you, it frustrates me that I got mixed up in all of that shit. Jacques and Raymond chose that moment to retaliate. Many of the wrestlers had already made up their minds and believed that all Quebecers were "Pat Patterson guys," and this incident didn't help matters. The fact was, as I've said, Vince wanted to control the Montréal market so the company brought in the biggest stars from Québec it could sign. We did the same thing everywhere.

I had heard rumors that there were issues between the two sides, but nothing to prepare me for what happened. When they pulled everyone apart after the fight, some people said I was in on it. I had to go to the Bulldogs and tell them I had no idea it was coming. It made me look very bad, and it was a complete coincidence that the Rougeaus and I started talking at that very moment. According to some of the stories out there, they used our spur-of-the-moment conversation as a diversion. Raymond Rougeau made sure I could not move in to break things up by holding me against the wall. Vince understood and he knew that if I had been involved, I would have told him. I will give Jacques credit for one thing: he threw one hell of a punch at Dynamite. There was blood everywhere. He almost broke Dynamite's jaw, and the Bulldog had to see a dentist afterwards. For a few seconds, it was hell on earth. That story became famous as one of the first backstage fights to be discussed publicly. I sure wish I had not been in the middle of it, just like I wish that story was something only insiders talked about.

No matter what, I've always known that being a wrestler is the greatest job in the world. I knew it for the first time on July 18, 1956, when wrestling brought 23,227 people to the Delorimier Stadium in Montreal. You see, I was there when Édouard Carpentier battled Antonino Rocca in the main event with Yvon Robert as the referee. It was a very good match, but in the end Carpentier got himself disqualified and people were booing. I was young and I was supposed to be selling soft drinks at that show . . . I didn't sell much soda, but I sure saw the match. From that moment on, I wanted to do what the wrestlers did: make people happy. That's probably why my favorite people to work with behind the scenes are those who share that kind of experience or feel the same way — even if they make fun of me about it unmercifully.

Mick Foley and The Rock always teased me because I would say nut instead of nuts, banana instead of bananas. I get excited sometimes, and I speak too fast. I'll never forget the night I gave Rock a suggestion for a match and finished by saying, "If you do that, they're going to go banana."

Dwayne started laughing.

"What's the matter?"

"Pat, there are ten thousand people. They're going to go *bananas*."

Sometimes Foley did interviews that had nothing to do with me and then end them by saying, "I know Pat Patterson would say this place is going to go banana tonight."

I had to rephrase some things so we could get some work done back in the days. Now it's funny; back then they were the only two laughing. So, if you've noticed there isn't an "s" after the word banana or nut in my book, now you know why. At least I know it'll make two people smile.

The Rock and I have a special relationship — I have been friends with his family for so long, and I've known him forever. I will always remember when he first got in touch with me about wrestling and said, "It's Dwayne Johnson."

"Who?"

"Rocky Johnson's son."

"Holy shit." I had not seen him in over ten years.

"I would like to meet with you. I'm in Tampa."

I had no idea Rocky Johnson lived in Tampa, or that Dwayne's parents didn't want him in the business. He had an in at the FBI but wanted to try wrestling first. When I saw him in action, I called Vince and told him he wanted to see this kid, not tomorrow but yesterday. They brought him to the office and he had a meeting with Vince and he was hired. His career was out of my hands from that point forward. I didn't exactly give him a job, but part of what I did was let the office know who I thought we should look at. And in Dwayne, I really saw something special.

When Rock was on his way out, leaving the business for Hollywood, he headlined a house show in Hawaii, the island that was his home for many years. He picked Chris Jericho as his opponent and they had a great match in a sold-out venue. After the show, we could not find The Rock anywhere. We finally discovered him under the bleachers, crying tears of joy. I am telling you: it was real emotion. We couldn't find him before the show, either. I finally discovered him outside, speaking to a guy dressed like a bum. It turned out that man was the actor Bruce Willis. We went to a party with him later that night — amazing things like that happened to me all the time.

One thing I want to say about The Rock: he flew me in for the premiere of one of his movies and I walked the red carpet with him. I can't even describe how special that was, or what it meant to me that he wanted me to hang with him while he was doing interviews. In the theater, I was sitting on one side of his mother, Ata. Then he came in and he sat on the other side of her and the movie started. After there was a wonderful party with food and booze. I barely saw him there — he had all of these movie people around him, talking about his new life in Hollywood. I gave him one final piece of advice that night: "Make sure you enjoy it."

With some guys, like The Rock, you only had to explain the essence of the business once, and they get it instinctively, and go on to enhance your vision. But on the other hand, there are guys you can explain it to a million times and you're never really going to get what you need. But it's your job as a producer to make sure the company's vision comes across anyway.

There are very good wrestlers who are never going to be the performer that Vince sees as *the* guy. The reality is: you have to convince the director of the movie that you're right for the part. Some guys are just not good enough for WWE. It's hard to meet with so many aspiring Superstars without letting down a few people along the way. I always liked to help the new guys. But I'm never personally on a mission, because if Vince doesn't hire them, there's not much I can do.

Over the years, I've just ignored all casting-couch innuendo made toward me and my work at WWE. I was smarter than that. It still hurts, but there was really no way for me to defend myself. I became the disappointed wannabe wrestler's ultimate excuse for why they weren't offered a contract. And that's just silly. People who were unhappy used the fact that I am gay to get back at WWE. To all the people who have ever said they weren't hired because they were not gay, I can only say, "Guys, I'm sorry. You were just not good enough."

On the other hand, just about everyone who ever made money with WWE loves working with me. And yes, even Sylvain Grenier made it on his own; he did not receive special treatment because of our friendship. In fact, it was in a segment where Sylvain was getting beat up by Chris Jericho that Vince noticed him.

Still, it always makes me feel good to speak with the kids training in Orlando with NXT. Can you imagine what a few words of encouragement can do? It's no different from when Kowalski or Maurice told me I was a good wrestler. We were all in their shoes once, and I remember what that was like. At the same time, I don't play favorites and I don't hesitate to tell someone when they're making mistakes. Everybody needs to hear the truth — even a WWE Champion.

I remember a time, years ago, when Hulk Hogan's punches were . . . the shits. He was leaving town for a show and I was not on the road with him, so I left him a message. "Terry, when you throw your punch, you need to put everything you've got into it. Know what I'm trying to say?" I left it at that. Apparently he received the message in the dressing room and told the guys, "There is nobody better than Pat Patterson. I wish he was here."

Everybody needs to be produced, and main-event guys appreciate when you take the time to tell them if something is not working. That's what made them main-event talent in the first place. When Shawn Michaels finally grasped everything I was trying to teach him, he said it changed his entire perspective on how a match works. It really clicked one night, when I told him to listen to and feed off the crowd. Next thing I knew, he was doing that every night, waiting for the crowd to cheer him back to life when he seemed beaten.

I fondly remember asking Vince about putting together an old-timer battle royal. He was sure no one would come because he felt they all hated him. They all came at my request. I caught some flak because I forgot about Angelo Poffo. A few days after the show, Vince told me Macho Man was going crazy because I didn't invite his father to participate. But before the show, he never said anything to me. If he had, I would have invited him without hesitation. The truth is his dad's name just didn't cross my mind. I called Randy and told him I simply forgot. He wouldn't listen to reason. So I said, "You're still mad? I'm flying to goddamn Tampa and I will meet you face-to-face. We'll settle this."

"I will be waiting for you," he said in his wrestling voice.

I told Vince where I was going. "Vince, if he wants to fight, he'll get a fight, because this is bullshit."

When I got there and saw him, before anything else, I said, "Randy, let's get a beer. How's that sound?" We went to a bar and started to talk. "Randy, I have so much respect for you and I also respect your dad. I guess I just didn't think your dad could still do it, so his name never crossed my mind. And nobody brought his name up. It's my fault, my mistake. But it's not because I didn't want your dad in there. Let's just shake hands."

He did some Macho Man stuff and then he "brother-ed" me and we shook hands — and that was the end of it. I never heard about it again in thirty years.

There is something else I need to get off my chest before I'm finished with this book. When Sylvain Grenier was let go, I was hurt. Sylvain is like a son to me. Some people believe I got him hired, but he went through the same process as everybody else, and I was not the only one who was in favor of him getting a contract. I don't bullshit Vince, I don't play politics, and I don't kiss ass. I've never told any of the talent "I will talk to Vince about you." I don't care if you like me or not, if you're good in the ring, nothing else matters at the end of the day.

But I do think Sylvain was put in a bad situation because of me. He was stamped as my guy, and that hurt him; he wasn't treated impartially. It stings. Over the years I've made my point often enough, and I've been proven right on more than a few occasions. I think my track record speaks for itself when you consider the Superstars I've believed in: men like Bret Hart, Shawn Michaels, The Rock, Rey Mysterio, and, even more recently, Daniel Bryan.

I've always believed that I have a responsibility to the company to say how I feel about something or someone and why. But I am not going to fight and fight for an idea to make it a much bigger deal than it should be. Even if my gut tells me we need to go in a certain direction, once I said my piece, Vince could decide whatever he

Working with Daniel Bryan is always fun, even with the pressure of WrestleMania.

wanted and I would respect that decision. But there are some wrestlers who have a hard time seeing the business like that. They find it hard to accept that we work toward one man's vision and, good or bad, this is the vision for the whole company. It's up to the rest of us to play our role. That's it. That's how The Rock made a name for himself in Hollywood, because he was so easy to work with. He understood his *role* in the production of a movie. *Know your role* is not just a catchphrase, you know?

It's taken me an entire career to understand that I would be a part of this business forever. In 2004, my last night was scheduled to take place in Milwaukee. I was burned out once more. And no, there is no truth to all those bullshit rumors that say I was fighting against Triple H being allowed to work behind the scenes. I swear, I'll never understand how that got started. That night, everyone had a big party for me, and Vince even had me sing "My Way." Shane and Stephanie came out, too, and I started crying. They gave me a big send-off — even Shawn Michaels, who was hurt, had a great match, just for me. I got a big ovation from all of the talent and staff. When I went back to the hotel afterward, I found myself sitting at the bar all by myself and that's when I started to cry like a baby. *What was I going to do now?*

I think I realized my life as I knew it was over. I don't remember precisely how it happened, but I was brought back a few years later after a health scare. (More on that in a bit — keep reading.) Somehow, they found a way to pull me back in. Vince's good at doing that — he had me come to see him at a show and he simply never let me leave again.

"I quit so many times and you always get me back," I said to him. "You're going to kill me, you know."

"Patrick, I'm going to get everything I can out of you. Even if you are on a goddamn oxygen tank, I will make sure to check to see what you think about our plans for the next week."

And you know, I wouldn't want it any other way.

Today I still work in the office as a consultant. I get angry when I see some of our television matches, and I think that's why they still want me there, to give them a point of view from the outside. And I understand how hard it is because I've been there. (Mind you, I've never had to write three hours of television for every Monday and then another two hours for the next day . . .) I understand the pressure. I know there's a lot to think about and that not everything is going to be perfect all the time. I think they appreciate my honesty, and the fact that I don't take it personally when my ideas are not included in a show. That doesn't mean I won't take five minutes to let Vince know what I think, straight from the heart, as always. I told Vince, the day he says, "Patrick, we're done," I'm going to ask him to stand and drop his pants, so I can kiss his ass and say thank you very much. Obviously, I'm playing a Jedi mind trick so I can stay as long as possible. Still, when he feels I can no longer contribute, I won't be bitter and I won't be mad. I'll be happy to have been part of that team for so long.

And sometimes I honestly don't know why he likes keeping me around. There's nothing for me to do because they're talking about stuff I know nothing about. And he just says, "Don't worry about it, Patrick. I always feel better when I have you around." I feel lucky when Vince says things like that. But he's also said, "You're not lucky; you deserve it."

Vince's mind is always busy. I don't think he has an off mode, not even when he's sleeping. If I were an asshole, or if I caused trouble, I would not be around. I'm that little devil or little angel on his shoulder who's there to point out the obvious. The things that, because he's so busy with other aspects of the business, he sometimes misses or doesn't completely realize we shouldn't be doing. I see the little things. Overall, I believe our show is very good, but I can still pinpoint some little things we need to improve. I know I'm not going to get an answer from him right away. I also know that just getting him thinking is the first part of the process. Once he's aware of a problem, he will take care of it. Some people think Vince is blinded by our successes, and that can't see when stuff is bad. But believe me, he always knows. He just won't discuss it with everyone.

He even appreciates it when I'm upset about a direction we are pursuing. But that's because I know I need to accept it, and because I make sure to help with all of my ability, even if I don't feel something's right. I make my point and then I move on. In fact, he'd get more upset if I told him about a reservation after the fact.

"Pat, I need your feedback. It doesn't matter if I'm busy. Just tell me."

And so that's what I try to do.

The whole family is there with me: Stephanie, Paul, Shane, Vince and Linda.

Everything is so hectic when we're working on our television programming that sometimes we just don't have the time to make sure all the producers and talent understand exactly what we need out of them. And so sometimes what gets translated from paper to reality is not quite what we had in mind. I've never been afraid to go straight to the talent and explain what was going on without sugar-coating things. I think the Superstars appreciate when you respect them by not trying to put a spin on something bad.

Like Michael Corleone, somehow they keep pulling me back in. I'm usually at television the week of a PPV and whenever else I feel like it.

And hopefully, I will be able to do this until I die.

THE FRUITS OF MY LABOR

"And now, the end is near;
And so I face the final curtain."

Each year, after a few winter months in Florida, I begin to miss Montréal and am eager to go home and recharge my batteries. After all these years of living elsewhere, it's still my home, and it is very important for me to go back and spend the summer there. I drop by Montréal from time to time even when it's cold as hell — I love that city.

Early on in my career, I realized you have to take life seriously, because if you don't, you won't end up where you want to be. You have to be careful — if you start doing something like taking drugs, you're going to fuck everything up. That's why I never took drugs: I was in charge of my life. I quickly learned that nothing lasts forever, especially not a wrestling career. I don't know how long I'm going to live, or even if I am going to be healthy in a few years. I don't want to end up in a home and rot away all alone, so I always keep an eye on the future. I didn't think Louie would go first. And with all the travel I did, I could have died in a car accident on almost any given day. Still, as you know, that doesn't mean I didn't have fun along the way . . . And I still have fun today.

I play golf a lot with friends, and I enjoy spending time with the likes of Sylvain Grenier, Stéphane Levasseur, and Frédéric Dumoulin. (I even sang at their weddings.) Don't worry, ladies, Sylvain is not married yet.

If I had not found wrestling, I might have become a comedian. Here in Québec, there was a guy named Gilles Latulippe who became really famous doing vaudeville, burlesque, television, and theater. After meeting on the golf course, we became good friends. If we had met when we were young, we could have become quite the funny pair. Strangely we were brought up in the same neighborhood — his dad owned the local hardware store. But he was almost four years older than me, and we didn't meet until decades later. When we played golf, we'd never stop telling jokes. During the summer, I sometimes went to Gilles's shows. He was amazing onstage, exactly what I think comedy should be. When he passed away in 2014, Gilles's widow and son made sure to let me know he appreciated my friendship. We laughed our asses off together, that's for sure, and it makes me wonder about roads not taken.

Another person I got to know at Le Mirage — the golf club owned by René Angélil, Céline Dion's husband and former manager — said to me when we first met, "Mr. Patterson, I know you very well and I know your real name. It's Pierre Clermont."

I thought, *What's the big deal? You're not the only one, buddy.* "Yeah, so?"

"I know everything about your whole career."

He introduced himself as Rodger Brulotte, but I still had no idea who he was. He said he knew many of my uncles, and that he'd been brought up in the same neighborhood, too. Well, it turned out that Rodger has been a Montréal journalist since forever. He was the French voice of the Expos and Major League Baseball when Montréal had a team. I didn't know that, I guess, because I had spent so little time at home during my career. He now works for some of the biggest television and radio stations and with the most-read newspaper in the city. We started to play golf together after that, and we've become friends. He's introduced me to a lot of the hockey players and other celebrities in the city.

I love to enjoy the simple pleasures of life and getting out for fun things like golf. But unless I'm performing in front of a crowd, I somehow always feel there is something missing.

One day, after finishing on the golf course, I joined the guys I'd been playing with for a beer at the clubhouse. I was a mess after a few hours on the course, so I just wanted a quick drink. I really looked terrible.

At Le Mirage that day, they were hosting an amateur singing event and the place was jam-packed. We went in and sat at the bar — but the thing was no one would volunteer to sing. It wasn't karaoke; you had to sing and people were intimidated. The manager started teasing me about going onstage, but in those days I hadn't really started to sing publicly. He offered to pay for all of my drinks if I got up. To make a long story short, you know wrestlers and their freebies. I got a standing ovation and after that two more people volunteered. I received a second ovation for my encore. It became a regular thing at Le Mirage and they always made sure I was going to attend on those nights. People tell me during the week that when I am singing on Fridays, they have to be there because their wives would not have it any other way. This really is how I got started and now people can usually find me at my favorite karaoke bar in Montréal or in one in just about any city I visit with WWE. There are even videos of me singing posted on YouTube — performing like this fills a void.

The first time I did a show in Miami, I was scared. I had to sing for two hours all by myself and I wasn't sure I could pull it off. People had paid fifty dollars for the show and a good meal, and I was more nervous than if I was headlining Madison Square Garden for a fifth time with Bob Backlund. Pier Béland — a famous singer from Montréal, who has since passed away — even got onstage with me as a surprise, and she never did that for anyone. We had become close over the years, and I appreciated her supporting me like that. Then Latulippe came out as another surprise and began to tell jokes. I never asked either of them to do this for me; they just did. People went away saying I had quite the show, and I was very happy.

Near my house in Florida, there's a bar called Frenchie's. As the name indicates, it's a favorite hangout of Quebecers living in Florida. I go there almost every day during the winter to eat and visit friends. I did a show there recently that I billed as my retirement from singing. If I ever come back to do another full show, it will have to be billed as a "special attraction . . . for one night only . . . as requested by the fans." I played my ultimate trump card that night to make sure I would leave an impression: I had The Rock join me onstage. The crowd went crazy when they heard his signature WWE intro: "Do you smell what The Rock is cooking?"

I fell to my knees as if I was truly shocked when he appeared, and then we sang a little duet. To close the show, I bought a glass of champagne for everyone in the bar and sang *"Quelle importance le temps qu'il nous rest."* Everyone in the room knew the French song; its title means "Is it important the time we have left?"

Maybe because I was born in such a large family, I never felt the need to have a lot of people around me all the time. I love a good party and everything, but I don't feel lonely when I am by myself. Louie has been gone for a while now, and I don't feel the need to be with someone for the sake of being with someone. I make many friends, but I'm free to do as I please.

I like going to the gym today more than I ever did during my active wrestling career. As I get older, I've noticed that when I skip the gym, it has an impact on what I can and cannot do. I want to enjoy life as much and for as long as possible, so I go to the gym. I love to walk, too, and that also makes me feel good.

I'm not a big movie buff, but if there is a can't-miss movie I will go. But it better be really good, because sitting in a theatre for two hours is not really for me. My favourite TV show is *America's Got Talent* — I *can* spend hours watching that. If I were a young man today, that's probably where you'd find me. On stage, trying to win a million bucks or become a star in Las Vegas.

I like doing crosswords and I like to read biographies. I've especially loved the ones about my favorite singers, like Frank Sinatra, Paul Anka, and Eddie Fisher. And I like reading newspapers to keep up with what is going on in the world. Back in the old days I would always have a book or a newspaper with me while traveling. Now, I also have my iPad. Surprisingly, perhaps, I like shopping. Now don't get me wrong, I like shopping, not buying. I usually just go to find and admire beautiful things. In fact, sometimes I'll go to a store three or four times before making up my mind and buying something.

I also love going to live shows. But it's mostly comedians who interest me, rarely singers. I did sit in the second row to see Alys Robi. She was a big star in her day, and if she was to come up today, she would be as big as Celine Dion. They made a movie about her life that really touched me and I remember her from when I was growing up. When I saw an ad in the paper that said she was having a one-night-only show at Theatre National I ordered ten tickets for my whole family. She hypnotized me.

I'll never forget that night; she was too good. I had goose bumps hearing her sing live. After the show she was in the lobby selling her CDs and meeting with fans. Man, I lined up like everyone else to kiss

I loved my trip to Egypt where I visited the Sphynx and the pyramids.

her hand. She was show business incarnate. And strangely, her dad was a wrestler — and she had dated Paul "the Butcher" Vachon, Mad Dog's brother. I remember her attending wrestling shows in my early days. She would be performing at Casa Loma and in between sets she would watch the matches at the *Palais des Sports*. My favorite song she sings is *"Laissez-moi encore chanter"* or "Let Me Still Sing Again." It touches me deeply; I relate to her being considered too old but she just wants the world to let her sing.

I still travel at least once a month with WWE, and I'm always wonderfully humbled by what life has in store for me. We did a show in Malaysia and stayed in Kuala Lumpur in a hotel just in front of the Petronas Tower. We were in a hundred-floor skyscraper, with marble everywhere, and I had a room so big I was sure there had to be a mistake. I was one of the producers in charge and it was shortly after 9/11. I don't have to tell you that security was a concern. (We also went to Singapore, where you can't throw your cigarette on the street without being arrested. There are undercover cops everywhere there.) In Kuala Lumpur, we weren't allowed to leave the hotel. We traveled in buses from the hotel to the arena, escorted by the police. During the show, I went outside in the parking lot and our buses were being guarded, with police cars surrounding them. No one could get near them — the idea being that they were preventing someone from planting a bomb. It's so odd to think back on it now, but things like that get you nervous about what could happen. How could I have ever imagined when I took the Greyhound from Montréal to Boston that I would end up in a bus in Kuala Lumpur under police protection? I didn't know what a Kuala Lumpur was . . .

When I was in Boston, I sometimes felt it was inevitable that I'd have to go back to Montréal. I was enjoying myself, but not making any real money. What was I going to do with my life? I didn't want to go back to work in a factory. I wanted a career. I was one of the lucky few who made it, but there was a price to pay. I missed the weddings and birthdays and — except for my mom and dad — even the family funerals. I was happy, but because of wrestling I was never as close to my family as I should have been. Another small regret.

Today I try to play catch-up. That's part of the reason I spend more time in Montréal now. I have a great place downtown, and in the winter I don't have to go outside and I can walk in the underground tunnels everywhere in the city or just hop on the subway. When it's warmer and sunny, I like to walk until I reach Papineau Street or the old Montréal Forum before returning home, just like when I was a kid.

I still enjoy the nightlife, and I try to make new friends.

I was in my favorite Crescent Street bar once when I met these two kids from Toronto. Obviously, they were older than twenty-one, but at my age, I call everyone I meet a kid. Anyway, I was sitting there hanging out, as I often do on a Monday night so I can watch *Raw* — I have a report to send in, even when I'm not on the road. Finally, after a while, they mustered the courage to ask me if I was Pat Patterson. I decided to have some fun and I said, "No, I'm not."

One of them said, "It's amazing how much you look like Pat Patterson."

"Who is Pat Patterson?"

"He's a wrestler."

"I'm sorry. I know nothing about wrestling."

The poor guys were freaking out because they thought they'd found my long-lost twin. They searched for pictures of me on their phones and showed them to me.

"Goddamn, that son of a bitch does look like me."

Finally, I burst out laughing and told then I was indeed Pat Patterson. I had an audience of two and that was enough for me. Again, if you ever meet me, expect the unexpected.

Another time, at the same bar, I struck up a conversation with two students about their future. They knew who I was, but we were just talking about life and about the future. I told them the story of my youth and they could not imagine how hard my early days were. We had fun drinking and talking. One of them gave me a big hug out of nowhere and told me, "Mr. Patterson, I will never forget you. All the knowledge and inspiration you gave us tonight. I want you to know, you made a difference in my life."

Another time, there were two women drinking beer on the patio when a homeless person passed by, grabbed their drinks, and started to run. I didn't think and went running after him. I caught him before he could even reach the corner of the street.

"Give me those goddamn beers now."

Everyone was watching, so I decided to scare him a little by telling him what I'd do to him if he ever tried that again. He ran off. I came back to the bar with the beers and got a standing ovation. Anything to get a reaction from an audience . . .

I love meeting people in show business, because we speak the same language. Most wrestlers from my day don't want to admit it, but what we do *is* show business. I don't go to a lot of wrestling conventions, but I managed to have fun one year in Las Vegas. I sang "My Way" at a karaoke bar and all of the old-timers in attendance were crying. I'm telling you, all wrestlers are artists at heart. In a way, I don't miss wrestling as much as some do, since I have found so many other interests and managed to stay involved in the business. But I don't want my whole life to be about wrestling, and I don't live and breathe the business anymore. I don't have a lot of friends who are still in wrestling. Mean Gene is a good friend, and he's still in the business — but more about him in a bit. The truth is, I used to enjoy the company of men like Red Bastien and Nick Bockwinkel because we had fun talking about everything *but* the business.

I have remained close with Louie's family and I go back to Boston once or twice a year. That's important to me. Instead of a tombstone, I had a bench in marble made for his graveside. It has his name, his date of birth, his date of death, and a phrase he loved engraved upon it: "I love loving you!" *I don't just love you, I love to love you* . . . I miss him very much. If it weren't for his absence, my life would be perfect. I don't know whether I want to be buried with him in Boston or back home in Montréal, but I'm really not ready to think about that just yet. Going to see Louie at the cemetery makes me happy. I feel close to him again. We're all scared of death; we all wonder what comes *after*. I don't know if there is something after, but it can't hurt to hope I'll get to speak with him again.

In 2006, I had a brush with death that changed my perspective. Actually, I'm very lucky to still be alive. I had an aortic aneurism. When that type of thing reaches five centimeters, they operate on you right away, no questions asked. (Remember that piece of information for a bit.)

I was in old Montréal with my sister Annette in one of my favorite Italian restaurants. For some reason, my back hurt like crazy. Nothing out of the ordinary after a wrestling career, however; it's kind of expected for your back and other body parts to hurt from time to time. I had played golf that day so I blamed it on a pulled muscle. I went to smoke outside and I tried to stretch, hoping it would go away. But it got worse. My sister finally said, "That's enough. You're going to the clinic."

When I finally saw a doctor, it was early the following day. He had x-rays done and everything. The doctor said, "It's very serious, sir. I suggest you go to the hospital right away with this paper."

I wanted to go back to Florida to see my own physician, but this doctor said I had to get checked out first. It was too dangerous for me to fly. At the hospital, I waited for quite a while before my sister got mad and finally got them to send me for a scan. At that point, I was suffering pain like I'd never experienced in my life. Finally, a doctor appeared to say that situation was indeed very serious and that they were waiting for a specialist. Twenty minutes later, after another scan, a heart specialist appeared to say he had to operate immediately.

"How serious is it, doctor?"

"You have a ten percent chance of surviving this operation. And even if everything goes well, you might lose the use of your legs."

I had been scared a few times in my life, but never like that.

I was able to give my sister my watch and rings and I said my goodbyes and I went for surgery. My aneurism was at *11.9 centimeters* wide: they had never seen one larger. People usually die before one gets anywhere near that size.

I woke up four days later, in rough shape. Even after I started to feel better, they still weren't sure if I'd lose the use of my legs. So out of fear one night, I just got up and started to walk, naked, in the corridor. I told the medical staff I was leaving to play golf. I spent two more weeks strapped into the bed after that little escapade. When I was finally able to leave the hospital and walk normally, I was told to stay in Montréal for another month to recuperate. When I finally saw my doctor in Florida, he told me he couldn't understand how I was still alive. A few months later, I went back to the clinic that had sent me to the hospital. If I had taken the plane back to Florida like I wanted to, I would not have made it. I thanked the doctor there for saving my life and we both started crying. I was grateful. Today I don't take chances with my health, and every six months I get a physical. Nobody knows exactly how the aneurism happened. And while my whole family came to see me and were very kind, it was no fun being so helpless. I feel like I've been given a second chance at life and I plan to make the most of it.

I have medication I need to take for the rest of my life, hopefully to prevent this from ever happening again. And so it's all good: I'm still here. Now that I have told the world I'm gay, I have more dreams for the future.

I would love to do a big show in Montréal, invite all of my friends to sing and play music. All the money from tickets sales would go to help gay youth. I'd love to create a foundation to help young people who have been thrown out or shut out by their parents, just like what almost happened to me. But I also want to say this: my father was a good father; we always had everything we needed. For a long time, he just could not wrap his mind around the fact I was gay. He met Louie and he finally came to love him. But there are a lot of people out there who are just as ignorant as my father used to be, men and women, who just need time to learn to accept their children. That's why I want to help . . . So no one has to experience despair like that.

LEGENDS' HOUSE

"And may I say, not in a shy way,
Oh, no, oh, no, not me,
I did it my way"

When I first agreed to be a part of the *Legends' House* reality program on WWE Network, I was not planning to tell the whole world I was gay. In fact, I didn't want to even be a part of the show when it was first mentioned to me. I said no without even considering it, but my friend Kevin Dunn kept the pressure on and kept telling me it was perfect for me.

I didn't know it at the time, but they wanted me on the show from the get-go. Sequestered in a house for weeks, with a bunch of old wrestlers, being filmed all the time, without access to a television, phone, or even a radio?

Hell no — and that was my final answer.

They kept insisting.

I finally beat the names of the other participants out of them — and that was only the first rule I broke on that show. I would be joined by Roddy Piper, Jimmy Hart, Tony Atlas, Jim Duggan,

Howard Finkel, and Hillbilly Jim. Mean Gene Okerlund was also going to be on the show, and that actually changed my mind about the whole thing. If he could do it, I could, too. He is closer to my age and I could have fun with and relate to him while we were in the house. Even Vince himself pushed me to do it. He told me I was going to steal the show. Look, I know they were trying to con me into it, and they ended up getting their way. They know me all right. And I did steal the show, if I say so myself. You know me by now, and it's clear I'll do anything for an audience.

But let's make something clear: *never again.*

I would never be part of another reality show, unless it was with younger talent like the NXT crew. I would not mind being a trainer on *Tough Enough* or something like that. I would like to be the Yoda character, the wise master, just like Chris Jericho calls me. Yes, I think I would enjoy that — but I would never be sequestered in a house again.

First off, not everything at *Legends' House* was about me being gay. It was no picnic, but we had some fun — and no, I'm not talking about performing as a Chippendale dancer in Las Vegas. The worst day of shooting for me was when we went fishing with Shawn Michaels. Four hours without catching *anything* — it was boring. And no offense, Shawn, but if Ray Stevens couldn't get me into that kind of thing, no one can. The worst part is when we got off the boat, there was a real steep ramp to walk up. The camera crew wanted to shoot us as we got out of the boat.

"OK, everybody ready? Get out of the boat."

They had cameras following us all the way to the top, but when we got there, they said, "We've got to redo it."

OK. So we got back into the boat and "got off it" all over again. After the fourth time, I got hot. And so I said, "Obviously you guys don't know your shit."

During Legends' House, I made a point with the production crew that they needed to pay me on our bet or I was done filming their scene over and over.

Doing that four times seemed stupid to me. But I don't understand the business of filming like they do . . . So I told one of the producers, "I'll bet you ten bucks you're going to screw it up again."

"Not this time," he said.

We walked all the way up the ramp again . . . and of course they had to redo it. So I told the crew, "I'm not moving until you give me my ten dollars."

They gave me my ten. And then we did it again.

The funniest story that made the air came out of an art show. Tony Atlas was actually very good. We should have had him do all the paintings. But I was doing all kind of shit, too, most of which never even made it to the gallery. We had the big presentation one night. People actually came in to see and buy our paintings, with all profits going to charity. This one guy spent $300 on one of mine.

"I bought the painting for you. I'm from Rio de Janeiro and you won the first Intercontinental Championship there."

I felt bad — and almost wanted to say something. Thank God it was for charity.

As I'm sure you figured out, I've never been to Rio. Even if, according to wrestling "history," I was there. *I have been just about everywhere else in the world . . .* For so many years on WWE television, they made it such a big deal about me winning the title there. I think I need to plan a vacation to Brazil, just to be able to say I was there for history's sake. If I do, I will bring the Intercontinental Championship with me and take plenty of pictures. Actually, that would be funny. Somebody from WWE should make that happen.

There's some good stuff that happened during the filming of *Legends' House* that they didn't air. Halfway through the shoot, Mean Gene and I asked for a day off. Two elderly gentlemen like us found the schedule grueling. It was against the rules, but we didn't care. I told the producer that we were either going in town to have a drink or we were going home. He told me that I couldn't.

"I don't care. Tell the others we are shooting something together downtown or we are packing our bags and leaving."

We were serious. We knew the company had invested a lot in the show, but we needed a break. They reluctantly accepted our ultimatum. And it was worth it.

It was about 5 p.m. and we went downtown in a limo. We were free — and it was great to get away. We went to this Mexican restaurant where there were a lot of older people — a lot of older ladies, in particular — having cocktails and stuff. My God, Mean Gene started chatting with one woman, and then another, and before you knew it, there he was talking with five or six of them. They were falling in love with him. He was telling them all kinds of stories. I was ordering drinks when I realized we'd already been there for an hour. I whispered into Gene's ear that I wanted to see if we could find a karaoke bar. I told him not to tell any of the women because, for crying out loud, they would have followed us. Anyway, I went out into the street and walked around and found a very good karaoke bar nearby. I couldn't wait, so I went back to where Mean Gene was, had a couple of drinks, and we decided that we were going to go singing.

Now, there weren't that many singers, but there were a lot of people watching. I couldn't help myself and I couldn't stop. I was in heaven. We kept drinking and just having a blast, a real great time. People were actually listening to me from the street and applauding. Eventually more people gathered to watch us and applaud. We were supposed to be back by 11 p.m, but it was already 10:30 p.m. and we were drunk. We realized we had to walk three blocks and I had to look after Mean Gene, who was staggering even more than me. We finally found a taxi stand, but there were no taxis. We waited and waited until I finally said to Gene, "Let's go have one for the road, across the street."

So we walked across the street, went to the bar, sat down, had our drink, and talked. It wasn't long before Gene looked around the place and said, "Patrick, there ain't too many girls in this bar."

"I know. It's a gay bar."

It was so funny. This guy walked by and I told him it was the first time my friend had ever been in a gay bar and that he was nervous. The guy told Gene not to worry; he was a good-looking guy and that they were going to take care of him.

"How did you become gay?" Mean Gene said to him.

"Well, my father was gay."

I couldn't stop laughing. That should have been on TV.

We finally got that taxi, and when we got back to the house, it was close to midnight. When we went in, it was quiet. The outside

Sharing Legends' House *with Mean Gene almost made the whole experience fun.*

lights were on, but inside it was pitch dark. I smelled a rat. Anyway, we staggered up to the front door, and I was afraid to open it, because I figured something was going to happen. But what the hell, we had to go in at some point. I turned the knob and the door opened. And that's when I heard Hacksaw Jim Duggan yell, "Jimmy Hart, you dumb ass. You locked all the doors except the front door."

They wanted to lock us out, but it didn't work. And when they asked us where we'd gone, we just told them. What were we supposed to do? They were mad, but they also wished they were the ones who had escaped.

And thank you, Jimmy Hart. Leaving the front door open almost made up for the fact that you got me soaked with cold water in that car wash in Episode Three. (Stop denying it Jimmy, I know you did it.)

That ultimatum thing only worked that one time, so we also tried to escape without telling anyone. Ray Stevens would have been so proud. Shawn Michaels had a big car to drive him to the house when he visited. Gene and I tried to get Shawn to help us by hiding us in the back. Not only doesn't he help, he stooges us off. Shawn Michaels, of all people! After all I did for him, Mr. Anti-Authority sold us out, and the production didn't even bother to film it. I think it would have made good television.

The *Legends' House* producer told me after the final show that it was "fucking good television."

If you watched the show, you know that at the end, we all shared something personal, something we never told any of the other wrestlers. I'm the one who actually started that shit. It gave us a great ending, a look at the real people behind the characters we've played. If I didn't bring that up, I don't know what would have been the show's ending.

The problem was that the legends were always playing wrestler for the cameras. They were in character, true to their gimmick, twenty-four hours a day, seven days a week. I kept telling them that the production wanted to know us, the real people that we are, and not just our characters. Jim Duggan doesn't go to the grocery store with his two-by-four. The late Roddy Piper didn't wear a kilt everywhere. You understand me, right? I didn't tell anyone what to do, but I opened up the door for us.

As I said earlier, I spent my life protecting the business on one hand, while attempting to keep my personal life out of the spotlight on the other. I'd been hiding something for most of my life.

The thought of coming out did cross my mind when I said yes to *Legends' House*. I thought it might be the place for me to let everyone know the truth. What I mean is this: while many people knew I was gay, I had never expressed it in front of a crowd. We had so much time to kill between what you saw on television and what was really happening that the thought kept coming back to me on a regular basis. By the time we reached the end, it finally felt right.

I realized the other guys also had things to say that they had never discussed, and that's why I proposed the idea of sharing something personal. It was like we all had something we needed to let go. So I opened up in front of everyone like that, knowing I had the right to let go, to be myself, without playing a character for anyone. For the first time in my life, I said it openly in front of everybody. And the most important thing is that I did it on my own terms.

I can't find words powerful enough to explain how important it was for me to tell the world I am gay. When it was done, I felt good about it — and I realize that's how you get to really know someone, with the truth.

Even though the show wouldn't air for a while, I didn't mind the wait. I was at peace with it all. But I also don't regret not coming out earlier — I just hadn't wanted to come out and I didn't see the benefit. I could only see it turning into something bad for me and the company. Even though Vince often said to me that I should do it, I didn't think the time was right. But in the back of my head, the idea was always there. Who doesn't want to be free? I kept telling myself that one day, I would do it, but until very recently, I never really had the time to focus on it. I shielded myself as I went on with my career, never letting anything or anyone get close enough to share who I really am with the world. A few years ago, I would have said that I never let it affect me, but today I realize it did. I needed to express the truth, and on *Legends' House*, I was ready to let go of the burden of secrecy. I was ready to live my life just like everyone else, no more hiding.

I had spent a large part of my life always playing a character. It was a good life, but I could never really be myself, never really let down my guard. Everyone knew Louie, sure, but I would always defend myself if someone asked *the* question. I would tell them they were crazy, that I wasn't gay. I knew many people knew something was going on, but as the years went by, people stopped asking about it. And I liked it that way. I never introduced Louie as my boyfriend. It was always "my friend Louie." I still can't call him my boyfriend. Somehow that feels wrong. He will always be "my friend Louie." And to me that's so much more than a boyfriend.

Everyone has something to hide. And no one really wants to be vulnerable on television. For us wrestlers, it's all about protecting our image and our character. The other legends probably didn't want to show that on camera; they wanted to project the image of always being strong. A few weeks later, after the final episode, Roddy Piper took me aside and said, "Pat, you came out. On the show. Thank you, from all of us."

"What do you mean?"

"We had an idea you were going to say that."

"So?"

"We support you."

Listen, I don't mean to be ungrateful, but I didn't want anyone's support.

Now think about it this way. I've always respected guys like Piper, Shawn Michaels, and Chris Jericho. They are small guys. I wasn't a big guy either, but I was different. For a long time, those guys questioned whether what we were going to do with their character was going to help them. It took them all time to realize they'd reached a level where it didn't matter what happened to their character. When I was producing them, I never made a big deal out of it: if we reached a dead end, I'd tell them to think about something else, that I would do the same, and that we'd meet again in an hour. Then they would come back with something new, or they saw the good in what we wanted to do in the first place.

That being said, still, it's good for every wrestler to think about what they are going to do. It's what the great movie actors do, too. They repeat their lines in their head until they can feel and become their character and give us a great performance. But later, when they go up onstage to receive an award, are they still that character? No, they're not. No matter how famous Sylvester Stallone became, he never talked to you as if he was Rambo or Rocky, you know what I mean?

When Stone Cold first got to WWE, he was cast as The Ringmaster. He hated the gimmick and eventually said, "Screw this." He went in a completely different direction. Out of that, a superstar was born. This is how you learn, by trying things. I tried many different things: Lord Patrick Patterson, Killer Pat Patterson, and Pretty Boy Pat Patterson. Various promoters loved those gimmicks, but that wasn't me. Even still, I made the best of them and made them work. But even if I was in the main event, wrestling for the championship, it didn't feel *real*.

I learned many valuable lessons doing this, however. Sometimes, people don't want to listen, don't want to change, because they've enjoyed some success. But if a promoter or someone in power sees something else in you, and if you want to learn, you should be open to trying new things. You can always try something else if it doesn't work.

Today, obviously, I'm more open about my personal life, even if I'm still a bit uncomfortable. But the great thing is, I'm definitely more comfortable with old friends. Angelo Mosca, the Canadian Football League Hall of Famer and former wrestling star, called me after seeing *Legends' House* and told me he loved me and that he had been moved to tears by the series.

I always loved Angelo when we were tag-team partners. I couldn't resist making fun of him, even if he could have killed me with his bare hands. He was so nervous one night in California when we were wrestling Peter Maivia and Rocky Johnson. We were in a little town in the middle of nowhere, and when I would tag him, I would trip him as he was climbing into the ring without him knowing it was me. He thought he was tripping on the bottom rope. He kept telling me he was sorry.

I called him recently when I learned he was dealing with the early stages of Alzheimer's disease. He told me he loved me and that he always would. He's a big man, a big monster in our business, and it never mattered to him that I was gay. It's been like that for so long in wrestling, maybe that's why people felt that my big revelation wasn't that big.

But it was for me, and it was for a lot of other people.

I've stopped counting how many guys have come up to tell me how proud they are of me and what an inspiration I am to them. I'm not used to that, since I was always making stuff up to hide the fact I was gay. It's amazing to me, but it makes me happy that it's helped. My favorite encounter happened in 2014 at *SummerSlam* in L.A. A FedEx truck slammed on the brakes in the middle of the street as I was walking on the sidewalk. The driver, who was a big guy, jumped out of his truck and came toward me to tell me he was gay, too. He gave me a big hug, thanked me again, took a picture, jumped right back in his truck, and drove off.

1...2...3...

"The record shows I took the blows —
And did it my way!
Yes, it was my way."

Writing a book about my life should have been easy. But that hasn't been the case. It's so very different from telling a story at the bar with friends after a WWE show. You need to say more than what you are comfortable with. If you don't, what's the point?

So, what have I been telling you? I'm a creative person and that's helped me to work with Vince all these years. Also, I'm totally different from the rumors and bullshit stories made up about me over the course of my career.

But my life has been a goddamn story all right — and recollecting it brings out a bunch of different emotions in me as we finish this journey through time. Still I don't want to say "I did it on my own," and I'd never want anyone to think I feel sorry for myself because I am getting old. Simply put, those things aren't true. Even if I live alone today, I've never been a lonely man.

I wrestled in all ten Canadian provinces and all fifty states of the Union and there is a story I could tell about almost every town and every major arena. Maybe I'll write a second book . . .

No way, never again.

It's hard to explain, but in wrestling, one of the nicest compliments you can get happens right after a good match when you walk back through the curtain and the guys come up to you and say, "That was fucking amazing. You were great. You are such a great wrestler."

It feels so good. And then it's over.

When the same people tell you to write a book, well, that's a different story. A book lasts forever. I believe that after more than fifty-eight years in the business, I was finally ready to write this story. Only now do I feel like I can begin to answer my own questions: Holy shit, how did I get here? I guess I was just busy doing what I love? Shouldn't that be the story of all of our lives?

I didn't speak more than a few words of English when I left Montréal and now look where I am. I didn't become a millionaire in Boston; I had a tough time. But I was wrestling every night and I was happy.

Roy Shire told me he didn't like gay people, but I changed his mind. Verne Gagne didn't like gay people either, and I changed his mind, too. By the time I made it to New York, Vince Sr. never even asked if I was gay. In fact, by the time I made it there, I didn't need to tell him. He couldn't have cared less.

In the end, being gay didn't really matter as far as my career was concerned. But I did, I think, change some people's perception about what being gay meant. I believe Louie and I changed people's minds because we showed them that being gay didn't make us any different than other folks. We were good at our jobs and we were dependable — just like any other good person. In fact, we worked harder to make sure that the fact that we were gay would not be used against us. Every day I was at the office working to change the promoter's mind. When I succeeded, those promoters would change the minds of their friends, family, so on and so forth. That's what my story is really all about.

There was no problem with a gay man working either in the wrestling office or in the main event of a wrestling show. If I did anything for other gay people it was to help change the way people see us. No wrestler ever refused to work with me because I was gay — I was a young gay man in the 1960s and I was successful. Kids today can make it, too; I'm sure of that.

But without Louie, I don't think I would still be here today. I would have gotten myself in trouble for sure. We were together for over forty years, and I want to make sure you understand one thing: he wasn't a professional wrestler, but he was much stronger than Pat Patterson ever was. He woke me up quite a few times along the way. He would tell me to speak up when things made me unhappy or uncomfortable. He was the rock in my life and I could always count on him to be there for me. As I've said, even today, I can only refer to him as my friend Louie. And that stings a little. We were hiding in plain sight for so long, and old habits die hard. Even though I'm out of the closet, it's hard to talk about it with just anyone. But I know one thing for sure, deep down inside, I love Louie — and he was indeed the love of my life.

Louie did as much as I did to change opinions, if not more. He was an amazing person — and a man who could also drive me crazy. He was always the person who would take care of friends when they were in trouble. He was loyal. He would have given his shirt — his life — for a friend.

Today in WWE, I'm the wise man in the corner of the dressing room who can speak his mind with everybody and anybody. The fact that I was beside Vince all those years says a lot about my role in

Teaching Superstars of today like Dolph Ziggler is very rewarding.

WWE. Yet, I don't want my life to be about how many champion-ships I won or how many *WrestleManias* I helped put together. That's Pat Patterson the wrestler. The man who used to be Pierre Clermont always had his feet grounded in reality. When I was not at work, I was not living in the make-believe world of wrestling.

I've had a hell of a life, and I must say before I go how much I liked most of the wrestlers who were in the business with me. We were all in it for the same reasons — they loved the business exactly as I did. Unless you have been in the ring, you can't really understand our bond. For me, it was like a big family, a real family. Some were the shits, some were good, some were great, and some were closer to me than others, but in the end we were all *family*.

My love for this business is a fire that still burns inside of me today. When you love this business, you try to get along with everybody, and that's when you can go out there every night and perform. I loved the business, but the business never took over my life. It was difficult enough just being me. I never wanted to be branded as "just a wrestler" or "just a gay man."

I live in Montréal for most of the year now. There is a little café downstairs from my condominium. I usually get there around 7 a.m. and ask the owner to make me my first coffee of the day and start my tab. While he fixes that for me, I take the broom and I clean the sidewalk, so the patio is ready for his customers to arrive. Sometimes I spend the majority of the day sitting there eating, reading, enjoying the sun, and making small talk. At least once a day, I make a member of the WWE Universe very happy as they recognize me and ask for a picture. A lot of the early work on this book took place at this café. I love Montréal in the summer. There are patios everywhere, and you can walk around and stop in three different restaurants in one evening. There are festivals and shows all the time. I love my city.

When I return from Florida after the winter, I like to stop by this little church. I spend ten or fifteen minutes in there — I sit and think about the future and my past, about my life. I don't know why, but it gives me hope. Churches in other cities are beautiful, but I don't react to them the same way. That small church in my hometown has always seemed to be there for everyone who needs it.

If I was starting all over again today, I don't know what I would have become. I would have had other options, I think. Maybe singing. Maybe stand-up. But all I know for sure is that I wouldn't be doing what everybody else is doing. Still, I would like to think that if a young Pierre Clermont was to show up at NXT in Orlando for a tryout today, he'd be offered a contract. Because there is no show business quite like WWE.

I was a wrestler, yes, but I didn't do that because I liked sports. I did it because it filled a void and allowed me to perform in front of an audience. Today what we do in the ring is arguably as much of an art form as any of the theater you can see on Broadway or any movie you can watch on the big screen. What we do is tell stories, and we do that differently than all other forms of entertainment while borrowing from all of them at the same time. What really sets us apart from the rest is that our audience is part of the performance. What they say and do influences what the match becomes on any given night, and it also influences what might happen six months from now. I really feel we deserve more respect for what we create each week and the joy that it brings to so many.

In French, we have a fantastic song that's been sung by many artists, including Céline Dion. It's called the *"Blues du Businessman."* There's a line in the song that summarizes both my childhood and who I still am today: *"J'aurais voulu être un artiste."* There's no perfect translation that really carries the emotion of what that single phrase means to me. The closest I can get is "I wish I would have been an artist."

I was lucky to find wrestling. Because of it, I became an artist. A real one.

I really don't have much of an ego — I'm here to help people fulfill their dreams now. Within the wrestling world, I think people know that. I've loved the business so much that I've never wanted to expose it. Even today, at a time when you can turn on the computer and read just about everything that goes on behind the curtain, I still want to keep some of the magic alive in wrestling. It just doesn't feel right to me to reveal some of the mysteries, so forgive me if you've felt like I was not telling you everything.

I have not written this book for money or glory; I've written it because I want to share who I am and what I went through with as many people as possible.

Those words to "My Way" that have prefaced each chapter ring so true to me. They're real to me when I sing them. And that's how you make a performance memorable; you discover the way the words resonate with your life.

When I was Pierre Clermont, I didn't know who I was.

Pierre Clermont is the kind of guy who would have worked all of his life in a factory.

Pat Patterson was a wrestler, a go-getter who loved doing what he loved.

I was lucky enough to be involved in this business and especially that I was able to help so many other wrestlers along the way. Not all of them appreciated my help at first, but they all ended up learning from what I was trying to teach them. I consider that a win.

The future for today's Superstars is bright. And I truly believe our business can only get better. To everyone who says the business will die one day: *you're wrong*.

When fans say I'm a legend it makes me feel good, but I've learned you need to remain humble. And if I was as bad as some people have said I was, I would not have been a part of WWE for as long as I was. I have made peace with it all. I love being around today's talent; I love the atmosphere at a show and the life of a dressing room.

The roar of the paint and the smell of the crowd . . . That's what we all miss the most after we retire.

ACKNOWLEDGMENTS

Pat Patterson

I can't believe I was finally able to finish this book! I was sure I would die before it came out! There are so many people I want to thank for their help in my life and with this project.

I would like to thank Bertrand Hébert for putting up with me during the process. « Hébert, je te l'avais dit qu'on finirait par l'avoir ce « mausus » de livre là. »

Once again thank you to Vince and Linda McMahon for believing in me during all those years. Thank you to Paul and Stephanie; as long as you need me I will be there. I would feel horrible if I forgot to thank Shane, even though we don't see as much of each other as we used to, you are family as well.

Kevin Dunn, my friend, thank you for everything you did for me and this project.

Here are a few more people from WWE who were an integral part of this project at one point or another: I would like to thank Steven Pantaleo, Michael Mansury, and Will Staeger and everyone else who made this book a reality.

Sue DeRosa-Cundari, a special thank you for your help on this book, and also for all the years we worked together — I could not have done it without you.

Thank you to Michael Holmes and the whole team at ECW Press for believing in my story.

Everyone in my family and everyone from Louie's side of the family, I love you all very much and I thank you all for supporting Louie and me through the years.

To Bruno Lauer, who wanted to know if he was in the book, now you are!

On a more serious note, a special thank you to my friends Bobby Cartago, Dorothy Hopkins, Bruce Prichard, Sylvain Grenier, and Chris Chambers.

When I think back on my life, I think of the many people who put me on a path to greatness: Sylvio Samson, Mad Dog Vachon, Killer Kowalksi, Buddy Rogers, Leo Voss, the Funk family, Mike Clancy, Danny Hodge, Pepper Martin, Roy Shire, Shag Thomas, Lou Thesz, Pat O'Connor, and Red Bastien. They all made it happen for me.

There were those who there with me for the ride: Ray Stevens, Mike Lebell, Jim Barnett, Nick Bockwinkel, Greg Gagne, Pedro Morales, Pepper Gomez, Rocky Johnson, Peter Maivia, Bobby Heenan, Lord Alfred Hayes, Jay Strongbow. Jack Lanza, Tony Garea, Gorilla Monsoon, André the Giant, Arnold Skaaland, René Goulet, the Brisco Brothers, Ric Flair, and Dusty Rhodes. You made this the adventure of a lifetime.

Finally, there were those I was able to help and influence after my career in the ring was over: Hulk Hogan, Undertaker, The Rock, Warrior, Bret Hart, Shawn Michaels, Ted DiBiase, John Cena, Chris Jericho, and Dolph Ziggler. Hopefully, in the years I have left, there will be many more so I can continue to share what I learned during my journey.

All of them played a part on who I was and who I became and who I will be. Thank you my friends. If I forgot anyone, I'm sorry. I'm no spring chicken anymore but it doesn't take away from your contribution to my life. Unless I left you out on purpose, then you know who you are.

This book would not be complete without a final thank you to the man who made me happy for forty years. Louie, I miss you every day and I hope you are proud of me.

"It was the best of times, it was the worst of times." These words seemed to apply to me at various times during the process of writing this book; but one thing is for sure: this book was the best of times. I can't believe how lucky I was to spend so much time with such a monument of the wrestling business. I have learned so much, I hope you will enjoy this book as much as I did putting it together. Thank you my friend Pat Patterson for believing I was your guy to finally bring your story to life. I will never forget.

Thanks to my children Zakary, Elayna, and Jean-Krystophe for understanding how important this was to me. I love you. To the rest of the family — my parents, Gérald and Françoise, my brother François (isn't that amazing I'm doing this?), Josihanne Daoust and Mylaine Lemire — thanks for the support.

Kevin Dunn, Steven Pantaleo, Michael Mansury, Sue DeRosa-Cundari, and Will Staeger and everyone at WWE. Thank you for making a boyhood dream come true. I hope I didn't let you down as I put my heart and soul into this project.

Micheal Holmes and ECW Press, you gave me my first break, I'm so glad we could do this together.

Sylvain Grenier and Marc Blondin, thank you for putting Pat Patterson and me on the same path, and for everything else.

Thank you to those who helped me by their research or by giving me an interview: Les Thatcher, Bill Apter, Tom Burke, Greg Oliver, Linda and Elise Boucher, Mick Foley, Gerry Brisco, and Dave Meltzer.

Finally, a heartfelt thank you to my friends François Poirier, Pat Laprade, Yan O'cain, Brian Shields, Rick Martel, Raymond and Joanne Rougeau for their support and help at different stages of this project.

If I have learned anything while writing this book it is that it's not over, it's only the beginning of another adventure.